AUGUST LIVSHITZ

TEST YOU CHESS IQ

Master Challenge

EVERYMAN CHESS

www.everymanchess.com

First published in 1981 by Pergammon Press (Cadogan Chess)
This edition first published by Gloucester Publishers Ltd in 1989

British Library Cataloguing-in-Publication Data
A catalogue record for this book is available from the British Library.

ISBN: 978-1-857744-144-4

Distributed in North America by National Book Network,
15200 NBN Way, Blue Ridge Summit, PA 17214. Ph: 717.794.3800

Distributed in Europe by Central Books Ltd.,
50 Freshwater Road, Chadwell Heath, London, RM8 1RX Ph: 44(0)845 458 9911

All other sales enquiries should be directed to Everyman Chess:
Email: info@everymanchess.com; Website www.Everymanchess.com

Everyman is the registered trademark of Random House Inc. and is used in this work
under license from Random House Inc.

EVERYMAN CHESS SERIES
Chief Advisor: Byron Jacobs
Cover Design: Horacio Monteverde
Printed and bound in the UK by TJ International Ltd, Padstow, Cornwall.

Contents

Introduction

DEAR reader! You are about to commence the tests in our second book. Unless you are already an experienced player, we seriously recommend that you first attempt to solve the positions in Book 1. The first book also contains useful general advice on how best to tackle the tests.

As in Book 1, each of the tests comprises eight positions which you are required to solve. We remind you that the tests have a time limit, and that each test has a basic evaluation of 40 points, with the proviso that you use the time allotted. If you use more time in solving the test, then for every extra 5 minutes you should deduct 1 point. If on the other hand you solve the test more quickly, then for every 5 minutes saved add 1 point. For an unsolved position deduct 5 points from your score.

This book is intended, in the main, for players of county strength, corresponding to 1st–2nd categories in the USSR (about 160–200 on the BCF scale, or 1900–2200 on the Elo scale).

As in Book 1, we insistently recommend that you write down your solutions. The positions should be solved without moving the pieces. Check your solutions with the answers only when you have finished solving all the positions in a given test. The time taken for a test should not include the time spent checking it.

As in the first book, all the tests are arranged in themes, for easier assimilation by the solver. We recommend that the combination solving should be attempted once or twice a week, but not more. Experience has shown that more frequent attempts are less effective. Practice has shown that it is very useful to look through a test some 2 to 3 months after solving it, in order to refresh it in your memory.

Over a period of more than 30 years the author has taken classes with groups made up of a wide variety of players, from novices to masters. There is perhaps nothing that arouses more interest in students than the solving of combinations. It is probable that a role is played not only by the aesthetic side of the question, but also by the purely emotional aspect.

And one further point to which we should draw your attention. Often the reader may find a line which is not given in the solution, i.e. a second method, which is also correct. In this case there is no justification for considering that the position has not been solved. However, if the new solution does not lead to mate, as in the game, but only to material gain, then your score for the position should be 1–2 points lower. If you do find a second solution, you should check it most carefully.

Your Chess IQ

A correct solution of all the tests in Book 2 will gain you 2240 points. It is possible, of course, to score more than this 100% total by earning time bonuses. On the basis of sample tests sent out to a wide variety of volunteers, we have compiled the following approximate table for determining your 'Chess IQ' in terms of a BCF or Elo rating:

Percentage score	Actual score	BCF rating	Elo rating
110	2460	210	2300
100	2240	185	2100
90	2020	160	1900
80	1790	135	1700
70	1570	110	1500

As in Book 1, we must emphasize that these figures are based on relatively small samples, and we would therefore be interested in receiving *your* results!

The progress chart

The chart on p. 115 is to enable you to record your progress. The scoring procedure was spelled out in detail in Book 1, and reduces essentially to the following: from the total evaluation for each test of 40 points, deduct 5 points for each position completely unsolved, and deduct from 1 to 4 points (depending on the closeness to the correct solution) for each partially solved position. This gives you your basic score, to which you should add or subtract the appropriate time adjustment, giving you your net score.

Editor's note

Note that 'W' ('B') beside a diagram number indicates that it is White (Black) to move, while '=' indicates that the player to move is aiming for a draw rather than a win.

Tests
1–56

Test 1   Positions 1–8

Time for thought 75 minutes. Theme: 'Double attack'.

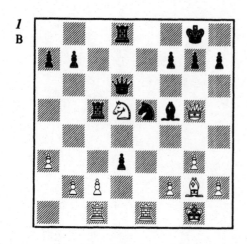

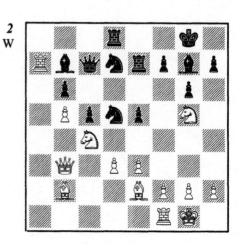

3
B

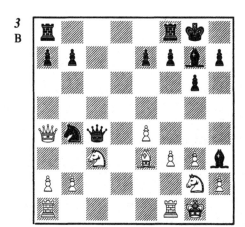

4
W

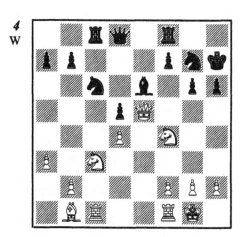

5
W

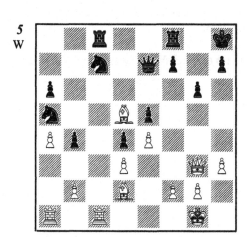

6
B

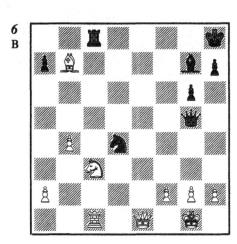

7
B

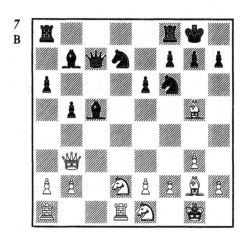

8
W

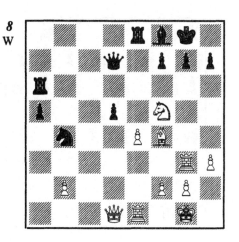

Solutions to Test 1

1. Karasalo–Stenoborg, Sweden, 1972.
   1 ... R×d5!! 2 B×d5 d2!! (*2 ... Q×d5?? fails to 3 R×e5!!*) 3 Q×d2 Nf3+ White resigns.
2. Panchenko–Loginov, Chelyabinsk, 1974.
   1 N×f7! R×f7 (if *1 ... K×f7, then 2 R×b7 Q×b7 3 Nd6+*) 2 R×b7! Q×b7 3 Nd6 Resigns (on *3 ... Qa8* there follows *4 Ra1!*).
3. Hamman v. Brinck–Claussen, Hastings, 1962–3.
   1 ... B×g2 2 K×g2 B×c3! 3 b×c3 Nd5!! White resigns (*4 Q×c4 N×e3+*).
4. Trifunovic–Kostic, Zagreb, 1949.
   1 B×g6+!! f×g6 2 Q×g7+!! K×g7 3 N×e6+ Resigns.
5. Minev–Larsen, Moscow, 1956.
   1 B×b4!! Q×b4 2 R×c7!! (*2 Q×e5+ fails to 2 ... f6!*) 2 ... Qd6 (*2 ... R×c7* is even worse, in view of *3 Q×e5+* and *4 Q×c7*) 3 R×f7, and White won.
6. Oszvath–Honfi, Budapest, 1953.
   1 ... Q×c1!! 2 Q×c1 R×c3!! 3 Qe1 Rc1! 4 Q×c1 Ne2+ White resigns.
7. Larsen–Portisch, Havana, 1966.
   1 ... B×f2+!! 2 K×f2 Qc5+ 3 e3 (on *3 Be3* or *3 Qe3* Black wins by *3 ... Ng4+*) 3 ... Ng4+ 4 Kg1 B×g2 5 K×g2 Q×g5, and Black won.
8. Keres–Gligoric, Yugoslavia, 1959.
   1 R×g7+!! B×g7 2 Qg4! Q×f5 (apart from mate at g7, *3 Nh6+* was also threatened) 3 Q×f5, and White won.

Test 2   Positions 9–16

We continue the theme 'Double attack'. This test is somewhat more difficult than the first, but you have some experience in solving examples with this theme, so the time allowed is 70 minutes.

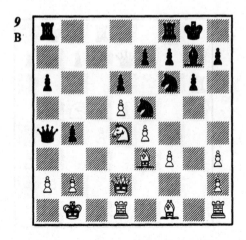

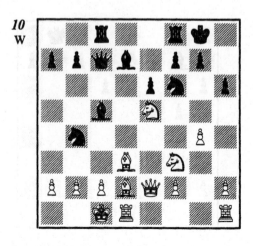

11
B
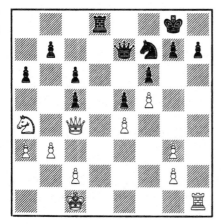

12
W

13
W
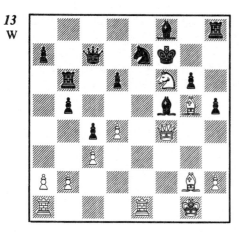

14
B

15
W
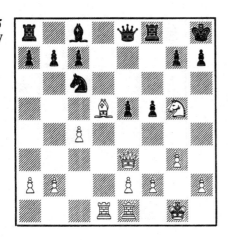

16
W

Solutions to Test 2

9. Zelevinsky–Mileika, Riga, 1970.
   1 ... N×f3!! 2 N×f3 b3! 3 a×b3 Q×e4+ 4 Ka2 Q×f3, and Black won.

10. Fuglewitz–Bernard, Corr. 1970.
    1 B×b4 B×b4 2 N×d7 Qf4+ *(2 ... Q×d7 3 Bh7+* or *2 ... N×d7 3 Qe4)* 3 Kb1 N×d7
    4 Bb5! Resigns. There is no defence against the threats of 5 R×d7 and 5 Rd4.

11. Solomon–Bernstein, Montevideo, 1954.
    1 ... b5!! 2 Q×c5 Rd6!! White resigns (on *3 Nc3* there follows *3 ... Rd1+*, while if the
    queen moves the knight is lost).

12. Stahlberg–Najdorf, Buenos Aires, 1947.
    1 Bf7!! K×f7 (on *1 ... R×d2* there follows *2 Q×g6+ Kf8 3 Qg8+ Ke7 4 Qe8+ Kd6 5
    Qe6* mate) 2 R×d8 Q×d8 3 Qb7+ Kg8 4 Q×a6, and White won. The game concluded
    4 ... e4 5 Re3 Bd4 6 Rxe4, and Black resigned.

13. Kording–Kassens, Emden, 1957.
    1 R×e7+!! B×e7 (or *1 ... Q×e7 2 Bd5+ Kg7 3 N×h5+!*) 2 Bd5+ Kg7 3 Bh6+! R×h6
    (forced, since *3 ... K×f6 4 Qg5* is mate) 4 Ne8+ Kf8 5 N×c7 Resigns.

14. Suetin–Kasparian, Moscow, 1952.
    1 ... R×g5!! (the immediate *1 ... Nb6?* fails to *2 Bf6+* and *3 Rd8)* 2 h×g5 Nb6 3 Qb3
    c4 4 R×c4 N×c4 5 Q×c4 b3!! White resigns.

15. Larsen–Nievergelt, Amsterdam, 1954.
    1 B×c6 b×c6 (if *1 ... Q×c6*, then *2 Q×e5 Q×c4 3 Qe7! Qg8 4 Rd8 R×d8 5 Nf7+ Q×f7
    6 Q×f7*, and wins) 2 Q×e5! Q×e5 3 Nf7+ Kg8 (if *3 ... R×f7*, then *4 Rd8+*, and
    mates) 4 N×e5, and White wins.

16. Euwe–Smyslov, The Hague/Moscow, 1948 (variation).
    1 Q×f7+!! R×f7 2 Rc8+ Bd8 3 R×d8+ Rf8 4 Ne6 Q×f3 5 R×f8+, and White
    wins.

Test 3   Positions 17–24

A new theme: 'Discovered attack'. For this test you are allowed 75 minutes.

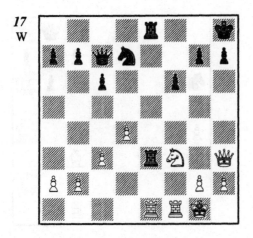

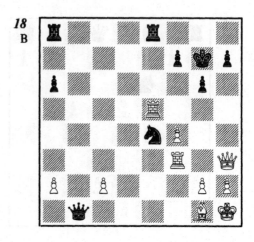

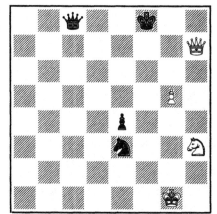

19
B

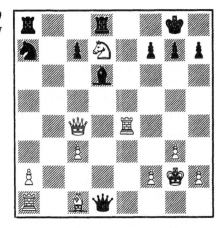

20
W

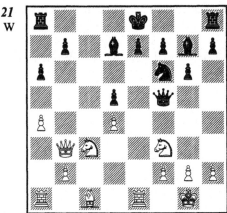

21
W

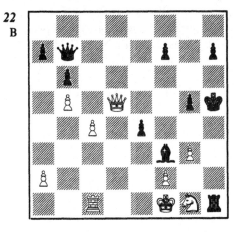

22
B

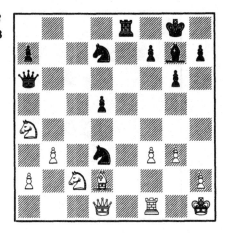

23
B

24
W

Solutions to Test 3

17. Zlotnik–Vasin, Moscow, 1962.
    1 Ng5!! f×g5 (*1 ... R×h3 2 R×e8+*, or *1 ... R×e1 2 Q×h7 mate*) 2 R×e3 R×e3 3 Q×e3 Nf6 4 Qe8+ Resigns (*4 ... N×e8 5 Rf8 mate*).
18. Walther–Tal, Zurich, 1959.
    1 ... Rad8! 2 g3 (*2 R×e8 fails to 2 ... Rd1!*) 2 ... R×e5 3 f×e5 Qb7! White resigns. Since if 4 Qg2, then 4 ... Rd2 5 Bf2 (or *5 Rb3 N×g3+!*) 5 ... N×f2+ 6 R×f2 Rd1+.
19. Ermenkov–Lanka, Yurmala, 1978.
    1 ... Qg4+ 2 Kf2 Qf3+ 3 Ke1 Qf1+ 4 Kd2 Qd3+ 5 Ke1 Nc2+! 6 Kf2 e3+! 7 Kf3 Q×h7 White resigns.
20. Vasyukov–Barcza, Moscow, 1962.
    1 Nf6+!! Kh8 (*1 ... g×f6 fails to 2 Rg4+ Kh8 3 Bh6 Q×a1 4 Q×f7*, when there is no defence against the mate) 2 Bh6!! Q×a1 3 Q×f7 Rg8 4 B×g7+! Resigns (*4 ... R×g7 5 Re8+ is decisive*).
21. Bronstein–Geller, Göteborg, 1955.
    1 Re5! Qd3 (*1 ... Qg4 2 h3!*) 2 R×e7+!! K×e7 3 N×d5+ N×d5 4 Q×d3 Resigns.
22. Kogan–Gindin, Kharkov, 1974 (variation).
    1 ... e3! 2 Q×b7 e2+ 3 Ke1 R×g1+ 4 Kd2 Rd1+, and Black wins. In the game Black missed this possibility, and played 1 ... Qe7.
23. Jones–Dueball, Nice, 1974.
    1 ... Re1!! 2 B×e1 (*2 R×e1 Nf2+*) 2 ... Nb2! 3 Bc3 N×d1 4 R×d1 Qe2! White resigns.
24. Stein–Haag, Tallinn, 1969.
    1 N×b5! N×b5 2 Q×c4+ Kh8 3 Qf7 Nc7 4 Bd6!! Resigns.

Test 4   Positions 25–32

The new theme 'Discovered check' is closely linked to the previous one, and is virtually a continuation of it. Time for solving this test—80 minutes.

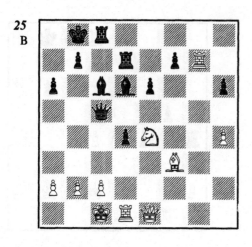

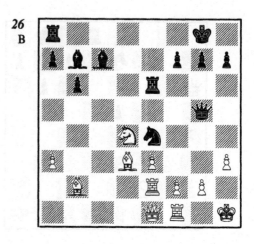

27
B

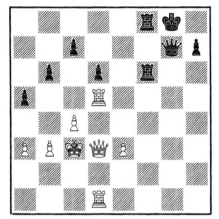

28
W

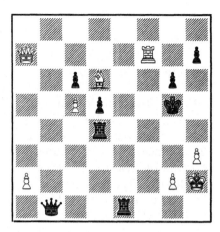

29
W

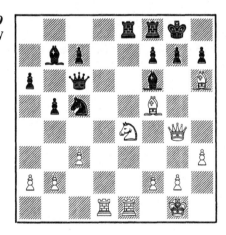

30
W

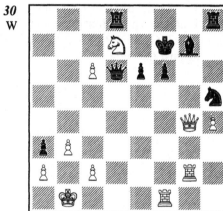

31
B

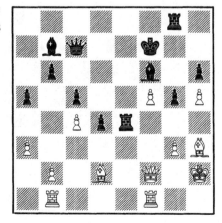

32
W

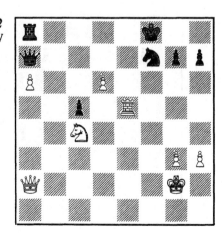

Solutions to Test 4

25. Parma–Bielicki, Münchestein, 1959.
    1 ... Q×c2+!! 2 K×c2 B×e4++ 3 Kd2 (or *3 Kb3 Bc2* mate) 3 ... Rc2 mate.
26. Muller–Wissel, Berlin, 1955.
    1 ... Q×g2+!! 2 K×g2 Rg6+ 3 Kh1 N×f2 mate.
27. Zita–Bronstein, Vienna, 1957.
    1 ... c6!! (*1 ... Rf4+ 2 Kc2 or 1 ... Rf2+ 2 Qd4 is less strong*) 2 Rd4 c5!!, and White resigned, since 3 Rd5 Rf2+ now costs him a rook.
28. Bunoch–Matocha, Gottwaldov, 1968.
    1 Be7+! Kh6 (or *1 ... R×e7 2 Q×e7+ and 3 R×h7* mate) 2 R×h7+!! K×h7 3 Bf8+ Resigns. The next move is 4 Qg7 mate.
29. Vasyukov–Kholmov, Moscow, 1964.
    1 N×c5! Q×c5 2 B×g7!! B×g7 3 Qh5 h6 4 Bh7+ Resigns.
30. Makeyev–Fomin, Corr. 1976–77.
    1 Qg6+ Ke7 2 Q×h5! R×h5 3 R×g7+ Ke8 4 N×f6+ Kf8 5 N×h5+ Ke8 6 Nf6+ Kf8 7 Ne4+ K×g7 8 N×d6 and wins.
31. Dayants–Dokuchayev, Liepaja, 1973.
    1 ... Rh4! 2 Bf4 g×h4 3 g×h4 f3+ 4 Kh1 B×h4! 5 Q×h4 f2+! White resigns.
32. Johannessen–Stahlberg, Stockholm, 1960/61.
    1 Re7! Q×a6 2 R×f7+!! K×f7 3 Ne5++ Kf6 4 Ng4+ Resigns. There is no defence against the mate.

Test 5   Positions 33–40

A new theme: 'The pin'. Time for solving this test is 60 minutes.

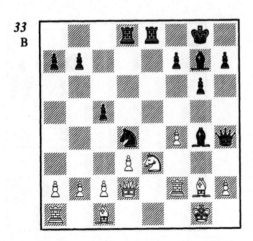

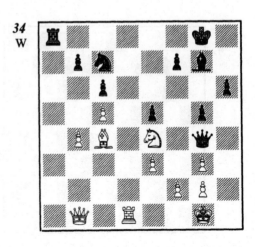

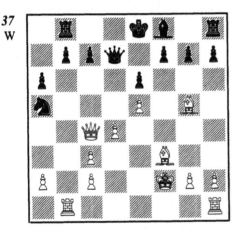

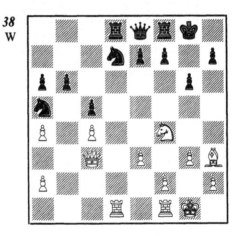

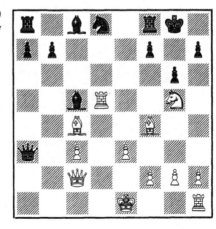

Solutions to Test 5

33. Barcza–Bilek, Budapest, 1961.
    1 ... R×e3!! 2 Q×e3 N×c2! 3 R×c2 Bd4, and a few moves later White resigned.
34. Smyslov–Fuller, Hastings 1968/69.
    1 Nf6+!! B×f6 2 Qg6+! Bg7 3 Q×f7+ Kh8 4 Rd7! Resigns.
35. Dahl–Schultz, Berlin, 1956.
    1 e6! B×e6 2 Bd4 f6 3 Qg4!! Resigns (*3 ... Kf7 4 Rfe1*).
36. Dieks–Lindblom, Groningen, 1973.
    1 N×e5+! f×e5 2 B×c5 Rc1 3 Qh5+!! Resigns.
37. Beni–Soluch, Hungary, 1953.
    1 Q×a6!! Qa4 (or *1 ... b×a6 2 R×b8+* etc.) 2 Q×a5! Q×c2+ (the game concludes brilliantly after *2 ... Q×a5 3 Bc6+! b×c6 4 R×b8+ Kd7 Rd8* mate) 3 Ke3 Resigns.
38. Benko–Fischer, Los Angeles, 1959 (variation).
    1 Ne6! f×e6 2 B×e6+ Rf7 3 Qd3!!, and White wins. The game in fact went 1 Nd5 e6 2 N×b6 N×b6 3 R×d8 Q×d8 4 Q×a5 N×c4, with a draw.
39. Liskov–Muchnik, Leningrad, 1958.
    1 ... Qg5!! 2 Qf2 (if *2 B×g5*, then *2 ... Ne2++* and *3 ... Rf1* mate) 2 ... Q×e3!! 3 Q×e3 Ne2+ 4 N×e2 B×e3+ White resigns. On 5 Kh1 there comes 5 ... Rf1+ 6 Ng1 R×g1 mate.
40. Portisch–Berger, Amsterdam, 1964.
    1 N×h7!! K×h7 2 Rh5+ Kg7 (or *2 ... Kg8 3 Q×g6+!*) 3 Be5+ f6 4 Rg5! Resigns.

Test 6   Positions 41–48

This test, as well as the following three, is on the theme of 'Diversion'. The tests will be quite difficult. Solving time—60 minutes.

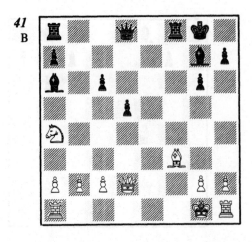

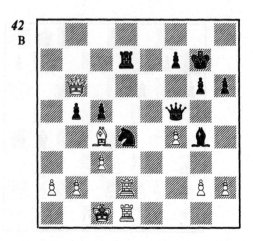

43
W

44
W

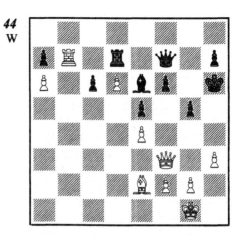

45
W

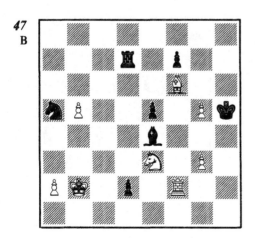

46
B

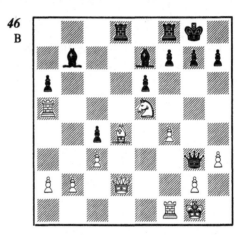

47
B

48
W

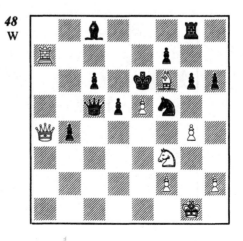

Solutions to Test 6

41. Iordanov–Spiridonov, Sofia, 1964.
    1 ... Qg5!! 2 Rd1 (*2 Qf2* is answered by *2 ... Qf4!* or *2 ... R×f3!*) 2 ... R×f3! 3 Q×g5 Bd4+ White resigns.
42. Driksna–Strautinsch, Corr., 1968.
    1 ... Qc2+!! 2 R×c2 Nb3+! 3 B×b3 R×d1 mate.
42. Khavin–Gufeld, Kiev, 1956.
    1 R×c1!! Q×c1 2 B×e6+ Kh8 3 B×g7+! K×g7 4 Qf7+ Resigns.
44. Tal–Dvoryetsky, Leningrad, 1974.
    1 Bc4!! f5 (on *1 ... B×c4* there follows *2 R×d7 Q×d7 3 Q×f6+ Kh5 4 g4+ Kh4 5 Qh6* mate) 2 exf5 Q×f5 (*2 ... B×c4 3 Q×c6*) 3 B×e6 Resigns.
45. Flesch–Paoli, Miskolc, 1963.
    1 B×e5! B×e5 2 d6! R×d6 3 Qa4 Resigns.
46. Bilek–Stein, Kecskemet, 1968.
    1 ... R×d4!! 2 c×d4 Bb4!! 3 Ra3 Q×a3! White resigns.
47. Solntsev–Vatnikov, Moscow, 1958.
    1 ... Nc4+!! 2 N×c4 d1=N+!! (*2 ... d1=Q* is wrong in view of *3 Rh2+ Kg4 4 Ne3+ K×g3 5 Be5+*, or *3 ... Kg6 4 Rh6+ Kf5 Ne3+* and *6 N×d1*) 3 Kb3 N×f2 White resigns.
48. Fuchs–N.N., Schwerin, 1955 (from a simultaneous display).
    1 Q×c6+!! Q×c6 2 Nd4+!! N×d4 3 Re7 mate.

Test 7   Positions 49–56

Solving time—60 minutes.

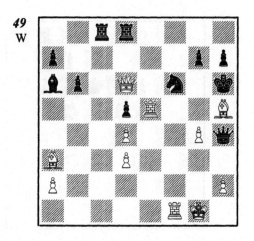

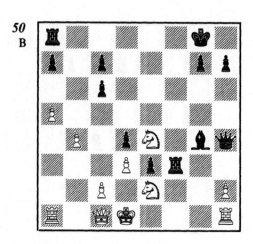

51
W

52
W

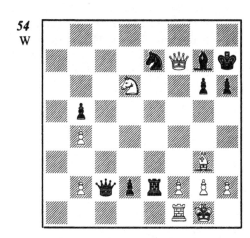

53
B

54
W

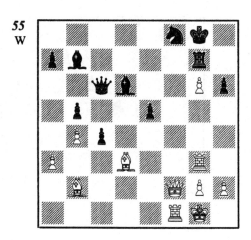

55
W

56
W

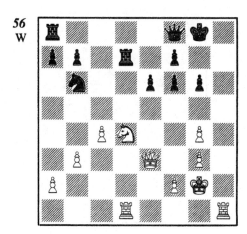

Solutions to Test 7

49. Yurkov–Gusev, Moscow, 1963.
   1 Q×d8!! R×d8 2 Bc1+ g5 3 R×g5 N×g4 4 Rg8+ Resigns.

50. Reifenberg–Hartlaub, Wiesbaden, 1917.
   1 ... Q×h2!! 2 Re1 Q×e2+! 3 K×e2 Rf2 mate.

51. Horwitz–Mayagoitia, Mexico, 1947.
   1 Qe1!! Qh6 2 Qe3! Qh4 3 Qf4! Resigns.

52. V. Zhuravlev–Koloskov, Corr., 1962.
   1 R×c5!! Q×c5 2 N×e6+!! f×e6 3 Q×g6 Resigns. On 3 ... Ra7 comes 4 B×h6+ R×h6 5 Qg8+ Ke7 6 Rg7 mate.

53. End–Podgayets, Garrakhov, 1967.
   1 ... R×b2!! 2 Q×b2 *(2 R×b2* is no better in view of *2 ... Qc1+)* 2 ... B×d4+ 3 Kf1 Qe3 4 Qc2 B×h3+!! White resigns.

54. Keller–Nievergelt, Zurich, 1960.
   1 Be5!! R×e5 2 Ne8! Nf5 3 Nf6+ Kh8 4 Qg8 mate.

55. Sandrin–Kramer, Omaha, 1949.
   1 Qf7+! Kh8 (on *1 ... R×f7* there follows *2 g×f7+ Kh8 3 Rg8* mate) 2 Q×f8+! B×f8 3 R×f8+ Rg8 4 g7 mate.

56. Bronstein–Ratner, Moscow, 1945.
   1 N×e6!! f×e6 (in the game Black chose *1 ... R×d1*, but after *2 N×f8 R×h1 3 K×h1 R×f8 4 Qe7 Kg7 5 Q×b7 Nc8 6 Qd7* he resigned) 2 R×d7 N×d7 3 Q×e6+ Qf7 4 Rh8+! Kg7 5 Rh7+, and White wins.

Test 8   Positions 57–64

We continue the theme of 'Diversion'. Time for solving this test—60 minutes.

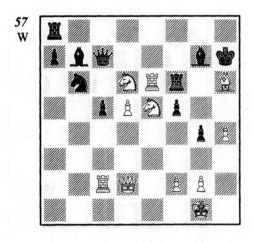

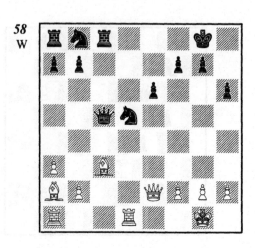

59
W

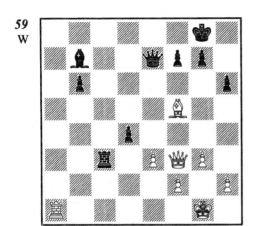

60
B

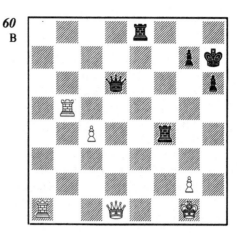

61
B

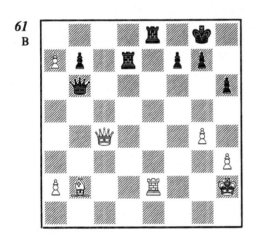

62
B

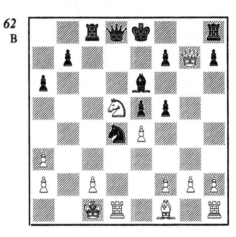

63
W

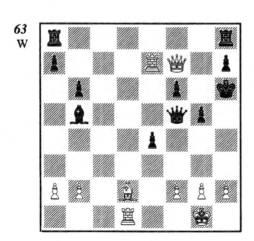

64
W

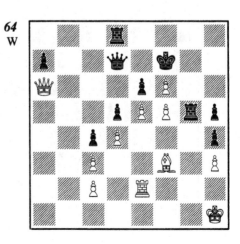

Solutions to Test 8

57. Vorobyets–Kogan, Lvov, 1974.

   1 R×c5! Q×c5 (or *1 … Qb8 2 B×g7 K×g7 3 Re7+*) 2 Qg5! Rg8 (if *2 … B×h6*, then *3 Re7+* decides, while on *2 … R×h6* there follows *3 Q×f5+ Kg8 4 Qf7+ Kh7 5 R×h6+*) 3 R×f6 B×f6 4 Qh5! Resigns.

58. Najdorf–Schweber, Buenos Aires, 1969.

   1 B×d5 e×d5 2 Qg4! g6 3 R×d5! Qf8 4 Bb4! Resigns (if *4 … Qe8*, then *5 Re1 Qc6 6 Rc5!* is decisive).

59. Almus–Herman, East Germany, 1957 (variation).

   1 Ra8+! B×a8 2 Q×a8+ Qf8 3 Bh7+! K×h7 4 Q×f8 Resigns.

60. Samuelson–Hilderbrandt, Halmstad, 1951.

   1 … Re1+!! 2 Q×e1 Qd4+ 3 Kh2 Rh4+ 4 Q×h4 Q×h4+ 5 Kg1 Qd4+ White resigns.

61. Wade–Duckstein, Muttenz, 1971.

   1 … Qc7+! 2 Q×c7 (on *2 Kg2* Black would have continued *2 … Q×c4 3 R×e8+ Kh7 4 a8=Q Qc2+*) 2 … R×e2+ 3 Kg3 Rd3+ 4 Kf4 g5+ White resigns.

62. Kalabukhov–Grigorian, Kiev, 1972.

   1 … R×c2+ 2 Kb1 Qb6+!! 3 N×b6 B×a2+ 4 Ka1 Nb3 mate.

63. Lewi–Zemlin, Corr., 1970/71.

   1 R×e4!! Q×e4 (forced, since *2 Rh4* was threatened) 2 Q×f6+ Qg6 3 B×g5+ Kh5 4 g4+ Resigns.

64. Rogozin–Laptev, Zelenograd, 1974.

   1 Rg2! Rdg8 (or *1 … R×g2 2 f×e6+ Q×e6 3 B×h5+*) 2 f×e6+ Q×e6 3 B×h5+! R×h5 4 Qb7+ Resigns.

Test 9 Positions 65–72

Sixty minutes are allowed for this test, which concludes the theme 'Diversion'. Since this theme occurs very frequently in practice, we recommend that you should once more look through all the examples of it; this will without doubt be of considerable benefit.

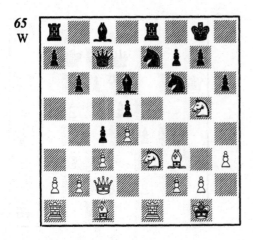

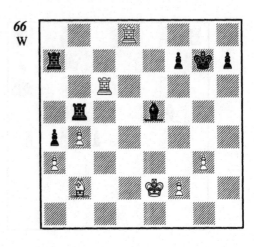

67
W

68
W

69
W

70
W

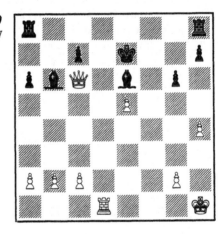

71
B

72
W

Solutions to Test 9

65. Ivanka–Kellario, Medellin, 1974.
    1 N×d5! Nf×d5 (if *1 ... Ne×d5*, then *2 R×e8+ N×e8 3 B×d5*) 2 Qh7+ Kf8 3 Qh8+ Ng8 4 Nh7 mate.

66. Panno–Bolbochan, Villa Gezel, 1971.
    1 Rb8! Rd5 2 Rd6!! B×b2 3 R×d5 B×a3 4 Ra5 Resigns.

67. Rubtsova–Milovanovic, Corr., 1969/71.
    1 Bd6! R×d6 2 Q×b7! Q×b7 3 e7 Q×e7 4 R×e7, and White won.

68. Tseshkovsky–Korensky, Omsk, 1973.
    1 Qd4!! B×c4 2 Q×c5 R×f7 3 Re1 Ng4 4 Bd2 Resigns.

69. Cortlever–Van der Wende, Beverwijk, 1968.
    1 Rf3!! Q×f3 2 Qg7+ Kh5 3 Q×g6+!! h×g6 (or *3 ... Kh4 4 Q×h7+ Qh5 5 Rh8!!*) 4 Rh8 mate.

70. Arulaid v. Duz–Khotimirsky, Vilnius, 1949.
    1 Rd7+!! B×d7 2 Qf6+ Ke8 3 Q×h8+ Ke7 4 Q×a8 Resigns.

71. Bouwmeester–Botvinnik, Wageningen, 1958 (variation).
    1 ... Rb1!! 2 Q×b1 N×e3+ 3 Kg1 Q×f3, and against mate at g2 there is no defence. The game in fact went 1 ... d4 2 e×d4 N×d4 3 Qe3! Ne6 4 Re5, and on White's proposal a draw was agreed.

72. Levenfish–Lisitsyn, Leningrad, 1946.
    1 Ra8!! Qc6 (*1 ... R×a8 2 N×e6+*) 2 Qf3!! Be7 (*2 ... N×g4 3 Qf7+*, or *2 ... Q×a8 3 Q×f6+ Kg8 4 Nh6* mate) 3 Ra7 N×g4 4 Qf7+ Resigns.

Test 10   Positions 73–80

Another important theme—'Decoy'. Like the previous theme, it is arranged in four tests. Time for the solving of this test is 60 minutes.

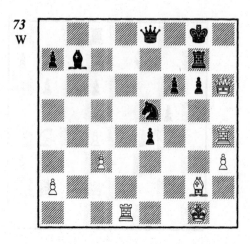

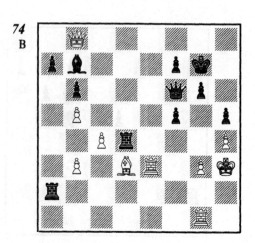

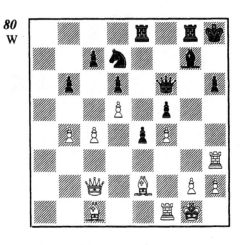

Solutions to Test 10

73. Szabo–Bronstein, Zurich, 1953.
    1 Rd8!! Q×d8 2 Qh8+ Kf7 3 Q×d8 g5 4 Rh6 Resigns.

74. Muryada–Yakubek, Corr., 1963.
    1 ... Rh2+!! 2 K×h2 R×h4+!! 3 g×h4 Q×h4+ 4 Rh3 Qf2+ White resigns.

75. Klompus–Vinklazh, Corr., 1958.
    1 Rd8+! K×d8 2 Qb8+ Kd7 3 Q×b7+ Kd8 4 Qb8+ Kd7 5 c6 mate.

76. Taimanov–Golombek, Stockholm, 1952.
    1 Rc7!! f6 (on *1 ... Rf8* there follows *2 Ree7 g5 3 R×f7!*, while if *1 ... Q×c7*, then *2 R×e8+*) 2 R×e8+ Q×e8 3 Qh6! Resigns.

77. Tayar–Bradley, Birmingham, 1963.
    1 R×c6+!! K×c6 2 Q×d5+!! K×d5 3 Be4 mate.

78. Westman–Gavanski, Krakow, 1964.
    1 B×d6 c×d6 2 R×e8! R×e8 3 Bf5+!! Resigns (*3 ... Q×f5 4 N×d6+*).

79. V. Zhuravlev–Kapengut, Riga, 1968.
    1 ... B×f3+! 2 B×f3 Rh2+! 3 K×h2 N×f3+ 4 Kg2 N×d4, and Black won.

80. Ratner–Pokorny, Moscow, 1946.
    1 Bb2! Qg6 (*1 ... Q×b2 2 R×h6+*, or *1 ... Qf7 2 R×h6* mate) 2 Bh5! Qh7 3 B×e8, and White won.

Test 11   Positions 81–88

Somewhat harder than the previous test, but it should not prove too difficult. Time allowed—60 minutes.

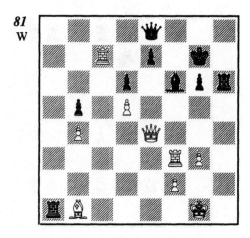

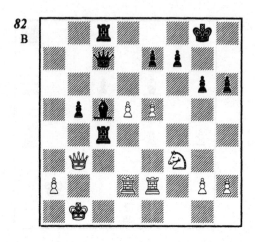

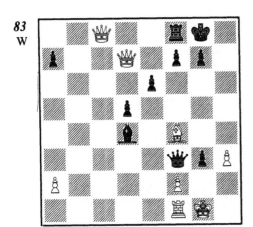

83
W

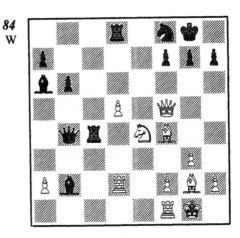

84
W

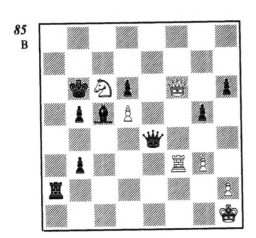

85
B

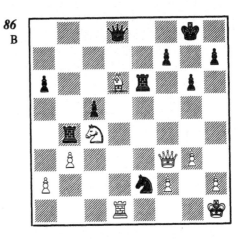

86
B

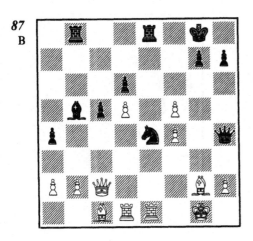

87
B

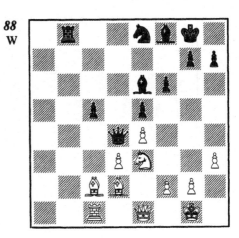

88
W

Solutions to Test 11

81. Stein–Filip, Moscow, 1967.
    1 R×f6! R×b1+ (or *1 ... K×f6 2 Qd4+*) 2 Q×b1 (not *2 Kg2 Rh2+!*) 2 ... K×f6 3 Qe4 Qf7 (there is no other defence against *4 Qe6+*) 4 Qd4+ Resigns.

82. Shugayev–Sevastyanov, Moscow, 1960.
    1 ... Rc1+!! 2 Kb2 (or *2 K×c1 Ba3++*, and wins) 2 ... Bd4+! 3 N×d4 Rb1+! 4 Ka3 Qa5+ Resigns.

83. Capelan–Bot, West Germany, 1970.
    1 Q×f8+! Kh7! 2 Qg8+!! K×g8 3 Qd8+ Kh7 4 Qh4+ Resigns.

84. Darga–Prameshuber, Graz, 1961.
    1 R×b2!! Q×b2 2 Be5! Qc1 (other moves are even worse, e.g. *2 ... Qc2 3 Qg5 f6 4 N×f6+ Kf7 5 N×h7*) 3 Nf6+! Kh8 4 Nh5 Qc2 (other continuations are no better) 5 Q×f7 Resigns.

85. Rubel–Usachy, Tashkent, 1962.
    1 ... Ra1+ 2 Kg2 Rg1+ 3 Kh3 Qh4+!! 4 g×h4 g4 mate.

86. Syakhov–Blekhtsin, Leningrad, 1962.
    1 ... R×c4! 2 b×c4 Nd4 3 B×c5 Re1+!! 4 Kg2 Rg1+!! White resigns. If 5 R×g1, then 5 ... N×f3 6 K×f3 Qf6+ 7 Kg2 Qc6+, and the bishop is also lost.

87. Furman–Batigin, Kalinin, 1950.
    1 ... Bd3! 2 Q×d3 (if *2 R×d3*, then *2 ... Q×e1+ 3 Bf1 Rb4 4 Re3 Qh4 5 Bg2 Rd4! 6 B×e4 Q×e4 7 Re2 Qg4+ 8 Rg2 Q×e4+*, or *2 Q×a4 Qf2+ 3 Kh1 Ng3+ 4 h×g3 R×e1+*) 2 ... Qf2+ 3 Kh1 Q×e1+! 4 R×e1 Nf2+ White resigns.

88. Pilnik–Pachman, Stockholm, 1952.
    1 Nd5! c4 (the only move, since *2 Bc3!* was threatened) 2 Be3 Qb2 3 Rb1 Q×c2 4 R×b8, and White won.

Test 12   Positions 89–96

Sixty minutes are allowed for this test, which is of similar difficulty to the previous one.

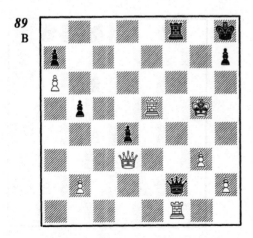

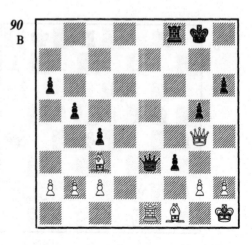

91
B

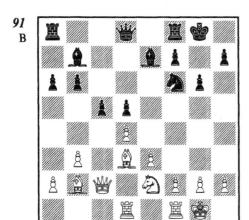

92
W

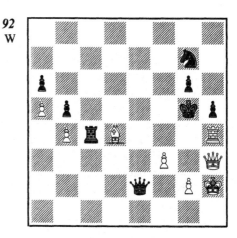

93
B

94
W

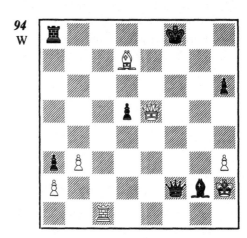

95
W

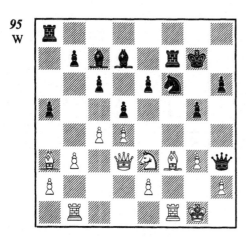

96
B

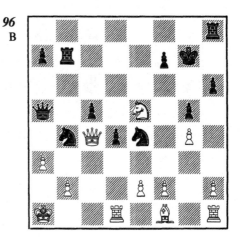

Solutions to Test 12

89. Ivanka–Lazarevic, Belgrade, 1972 (variation).
   1 ... Rg8+ 2 Kh6 Q×h2+ 3 Rh5 Qd2+!! 4 Q×d2 Rg6 mate. Black in fact played 1 ... Q×f1, and the game ended in a draw.
90. Vodopyanov–Kaptsin, Rostov, 1974.
   1 ... Qg1+!! 2 K×g1 f2+ 3 Kh1 f×e1=Q 4 B×e1 R×f1 mate.
91. Kozma–Korchnoi, Lukhachovitsy, 1972.
   1 ... c4!! 2 b×c4 d×c4 3 Q×c4 (*3 B×c4 Rc8!*) 3 ... Rc8 4 Qb3 Bd5! White resigns (after *5 Qa4 b5 6 Q×a6 Ra8 7 Q×b5 Ra5!* he loses his queen).
92. Jung–Szabados, Reggio Emilia, 1952.
   1 B×g7!! R×h4 2 Q×h4+! K×h4 3 Bf6+ g5 4 Bc3! Qf2 5 Be5!, and wins, since Black is in zugzwang.
93. Kluger–Pribyl, Olomouc, 1974.
   1 ... Nf3+! 2 g×f3 Rh1+ 3 Kg3 Rag1+ 4 Kf4 R×h4 mate.
94. Kudryashov–Zakharov, Tbilisi, 1973.
   1 Rc2!! Q×c2 2 Qf6+ Kg8 3 Be6+ Kh7 4 Bf5+ Resigns.
95. Lengyel–Pogats, Budapest, 1964.
   1 Bg4! N×g4 2 R×f7+ K×f7 3 Qh7+ Kf6 (or *3 ... Ke8 4 Qg8* mate) 4 Be7 mate.
96. Porral–Burgalat, Santa Fe, 1945.
   1 ... Nc3!! 2 Rc1 Q×a3+!! 3 b×a3 Nc2+!! 4 R×c2 Rb1 mate.

Test 13   Positions 97–104

The last test of the theme of 'Decoy', and rather more difficult than the previous ones. The time allowed is 60 minutes. Here again we repeat our advice to the reader: look through all the examples on this theme. In your practical play you will be able to appreciate the value of our advice.

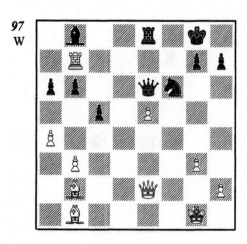

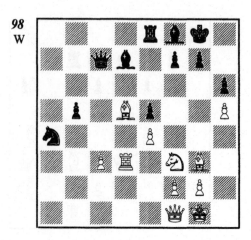

99
W

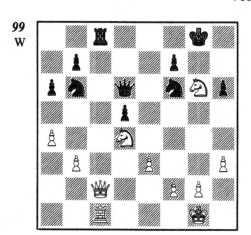

100
W

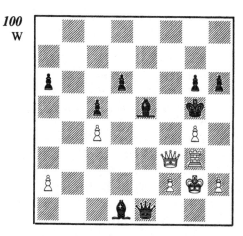

101
B

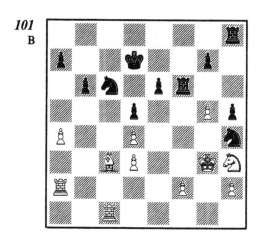

102
W

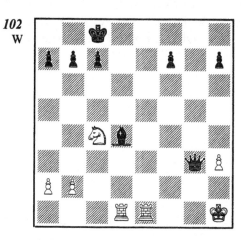

103
W

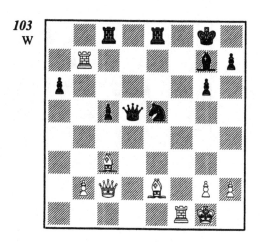

104
W

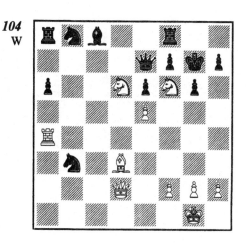

Solutions to Test 13

97. Böök–Koponen, Helsinki, 1961.
   1 e×f6! Q×e2 2 f7+ Kh8 3 B×g7+!! K×g7 4 f×e8=Q+ Resigns.

98. Matulovic–Lengyel, Vrnjacka Banja, 1966 (variation).
   1 B×e5!! R×e5 2 B×f7+ K×f7 3 R×d7+! Q×d7 4 N×e5+, and White wins. The game in fact went 1 ... Qc8 2 Bd4, when White remained a pawn up and went on to win.
   1 Q×c8+!! N×c8 2 R×c8+ Kh7 3 Rh8+! K×g6 4 R×h6+ Resigns.

100. Zhilinsky–Zhulanov, USSR, 1958.
   1 h4+!! K×h4 2 Rh3+ Kg5 3 Rh5+!! g×h5 4 Qf5+ Kh4 5 Q×h5 mate.

101. Bruckner–Koch, Berlin, 1952.
   1 ... Rf3+!! 2 K×h4 Ne7! 3 g6 N×g6+ 4 Kg5 Rh6!! White resigns.

102. Kofman–Sakketi, Corr., 1948 (variation).
   1 Re8+! Kd7 2 Re3!! Qg7 3 R×d4+! Q×d4 4 Rd3! Q×d3 5 Ne5+, and White wins. In the game Kofman could find no defence against 1 ... Q×h3+, and resigned.

103. Taimanov–N.N., Riga, 1964 (from a simultaneous display).
   1 Bc4! Q×c4 2 R×g7+! Kh8 3 B×e5! Q×c2 4 Rf8+!! R×f8 5 R×g6+ Resigns.

104. Veresov–Kukharev, Minsk, 1959.
   1 Qh6+!! K×h6 2 Rh4+ Kg5 3 f4+!! K×h4 4 g3+ Kh3 5 Bf1 mate.

Test 14   Positions 105–112

A new theme: 'Interference'. You should not find the test too difficult. Solving time—70 minutes.

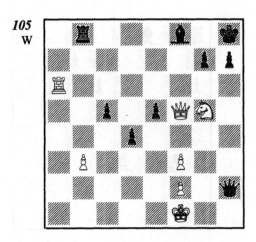

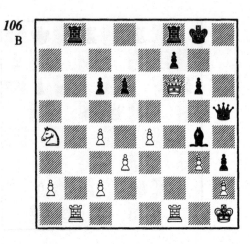

107
W

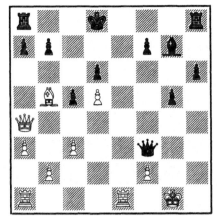

108
W

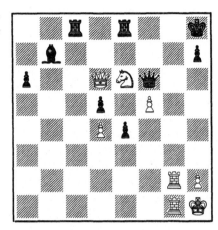

109
W

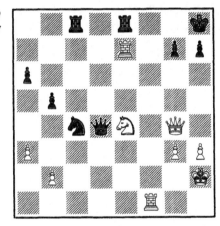

110
B

111
B

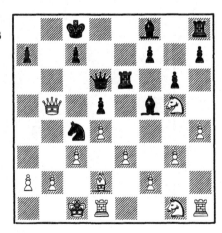

112
B

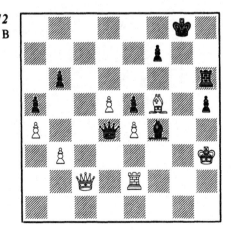

Solutions to Test 14

105. Kireyev–Mironov, Riga, 1963.
   1 Rh6!! Q×h6 2 Nf7+ Kg8 3 N×h6+ g×h6 4 Qe6+ Resigns.
106. N. Zhuravlev–Kapanadze, Tbilisi, 1977.
   1 ... R×b1 2 R×b1 Bf5!! and wins.
107. Augustin–Lanc, Brno, 1975.
   1 Be8! Qf5 2 Re6!! Resigns.
108. Ruster–Olland, Corr., 1968.
   1 Nf8!! Qf7 (if *1 ... Q×f8* or *1 ... R×f8*, then *2 Rg8+*) 2 Qf6+! Q×f6 3 Rg8 mate.
109. Cornflit–Hukel, Corr., 1965.
   1 Nf6!! Q×b2+ (or *1 ... Q×g4 2 N×e8!!*) 2 Kh1 Rg8 3 Qe4! Resigns.
110. Chakhoyan–Turkestanishvili, Tbilisi, 1971.
   1 ... Qd3!! 2 Q×d3 e×d3 3 Rb1 B×g4 White resigns.
111. Daskalov–Stancev, Varna, 1968.
   1 ... Qa3!! 2 N×e6 (or *2 b×a3 B×a3* mate, while at the same time White has to parry the threat of *2 ... Rb6*) 2 ... Bb4!! 3 Q×b4 Q×a2 White resigns.
112. Kasperovich–Bukhman, Moscow, 1977.
   1 ... Rg6!! 2 B×g6 (in the game White resigned after *2 Rg2 Qe3+ 3 Kh4 Bg5+*) 2 ... Qg1 3 B×f7+ Kh7!, and Black wins after 4 Bg6+ Kh6! or 4 Bg8+ Kh8!

Test 15   Positions 113–120

Sixty minutes are allowed for this test, which concludes the theme 'Interference'. Several of these examples may cause you to rack your brains.

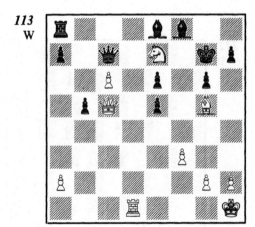

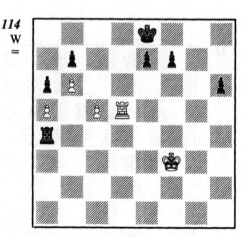

Can White save the game?

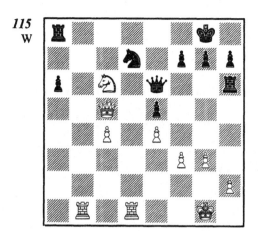

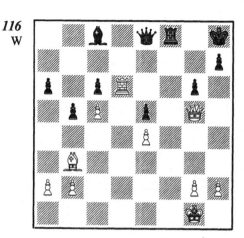

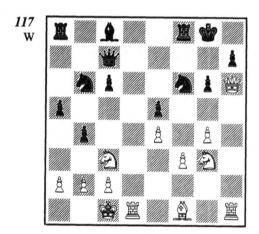

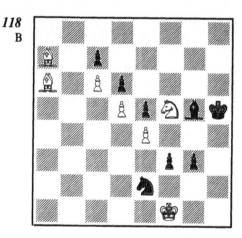

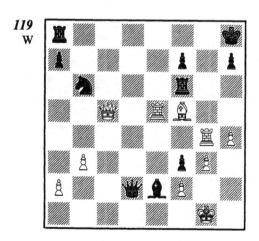

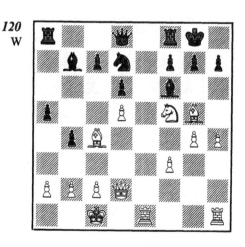

Solutions to Test 15

113. Gligoric–Szabo, Venice, 1949 (variation).
     1 Rd6!! B×e7 2 B×e7 Q×e7 3 Rd7!!, and White wins.
114. Eberle–Navarovszky, Budapest, 1959.
     1 c6! b×c6 2 Rb5!! a×b5 3 b7 R×a5 4 b8=Q+, and the game ended in a draw.
115. Bubnov–Yaroslavtsev, Voronezh, 1949.
     1 Nb8!! Nf6 (no better is *1 ... Nf8 2 Rd8, 1 ... R×b8 2 R×b8+ N×b8 2 Rd8+*, or *1 ... Qh3 2 Rb2!*) *2 Rd8+ Ne8 3 Rb6!!* Resigns.
116. Liskov–Baranov, Yuzhno-Sakhalinsk, 1950
     1 Re6!! B×e6 2 Q×e5+ Kg8 3 B×e6+ Rf7 4 Qf6! Resigns.
117. Wach–Gonsirowski, Warsaw, 1974.
     1 Na4! Be6 (if *1 ... N×a4*, then *2 Bc4+ Rf7 3 g5!*) *2 Nc5! B×a2 2 g5 Ne8 4 Rd7!!* Resigns.
118. Matushkin–Shumilov, Corr., 1973/74.
     1 ... g2+! 2 Ke1 Bd2+!! 3 K×d2 Nd4 4 N×d4 g1=Q, and Black won. There followed *5 Nb5 Qa1! 6 N×c7 Qa5+*, and White resigned.
119. Van Scheltinga–Orban, Amsterdam, 1954.
     1 Bc8!! Qd8 (*2 Re8 mate* was threatened, and on *1 ... R×c8* there follows *2 Q×c8+! N×c8 3 Re8 mate*) *2 Qc3!* (creating a new threat, e.g. *2 ... R×c8 3 Re8+ Q×e8 4 Q×f6 mate*) *2 ... Bb5 3 Reg5!* (with the new threat of *4 Rg8+* and *5 Q×f6*, mating) *3 ... Nd5 4 R×d5!* Resigns [*2 Qd4!* looks even stronger—editor's note].
120. A. Petrosian–Gusev, Riga, 1968.
     1 Re7!! Kh8 (not the strongest, but other moves also lose, e.g. *1 ... B×e7 2 N×e7+ Kh8 3 Ng6+*, or *2 B×e7 Qe8 3 Qg5 g6 4 Qh6 g×f5 5 g×f5*, with a mating attack; *1 ... Bc8* was best, on which there comes *2 Bb5 Ne5 3 B×f6 g×f6 4 Bd7!! B×d7 5 R×d7 Q×d7 6 Qh6*) *2 R×d7 B×b2+ 3 K×b2 Q×d7 4 Bf6!* Resigns.

Test 16   Positions 121–128

We begin the theme 'Defence-elimination' with a test which should not cause you too much trouble. Solving time—50 minutes.

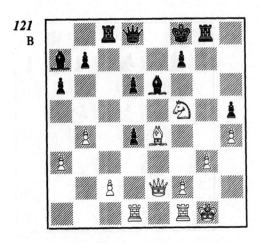

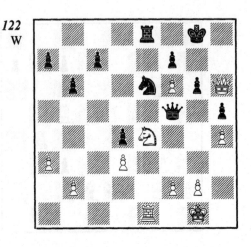

123
B

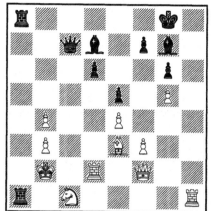

124
W

125
W

126
W

127
W

128
W

Solutions to Test 16

121. Donner–Keres, Zurich, 1959.
    1 ... B×f5! White resigns (after *2 B×f5 R×g3+ 3 f×g3 d3+* he loses his queen).
122. Polugayevsky–Gulko, Yerevan, 1975.
    1 Nd6!! Resigns (*1 ... c×d6 2 R×e6!*).
123. Varnusz–Honfi, Budapest, 1961.
    1 ... Q×c1+!! 2 R×c1 R8a2+ White resigns (since if *3 Kc3 R×c1+ 4 Kd3 Bb5* mate, or *4 Rc2 R×c2+ 5 Q×c2 R×c2+*).
124. Kochiev–Lederman, Le Harve, 1977.
    1 Nf4! Bb4 2 Q×b4! Resigns (*2 ... R×b4 3 Ng6+ Kh7 4 Ndf8* mate).
125. Pitlyakowski–Szuksta, Warsaw, 1952.
    1 Q×h4+!! B×h4 2 Bg7+ Kh5 3 g4 mate.
126. Schuppler–Genig, Mannheim, 1948.
    1 Bh6!! R×h6 2 Q×d4!! e×d4 3 Rfb1! Resigns.
127. Hübner–Siaperas, Athens, 1969.
    1 N×a5! R×a5 2 B×a5! Q×a5 3 a4 Ba6 4 Q×c6+ Resigns.
128. Mironovich–Goryaev, USSR, 1977 (variation).
    1 Q×d5! R×d5 2 N×f6+ Kh8 3 Bg5+! (the game ended in a draw after *3 Bf4+ Kg7 4 B×c7? K×f6*, although *4 N×d5!* would still have won) 3 ... Kg7 4 Rh7+ Kf8 5 Rh8+ Ke7 6 N×d5++ and wins.

Test 17   Positions 129–136

Continuation of the theme 'Defence-elimination'. Seventy minutes are allowed for this test, which is rather more difficult than the previous one.

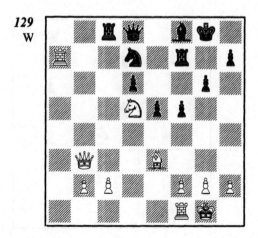

129
W

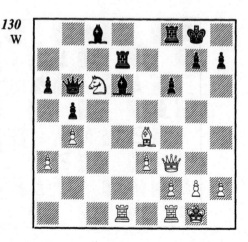

130
W

131
W
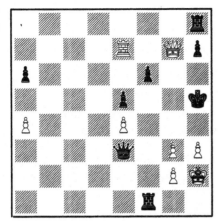

132
W
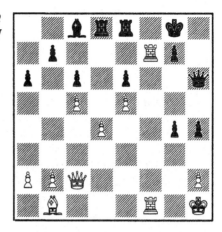

133
W
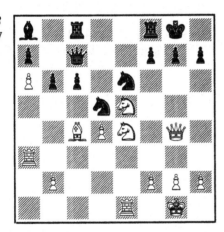

134
W
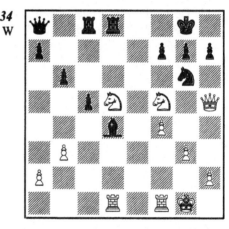

135
W

136
W
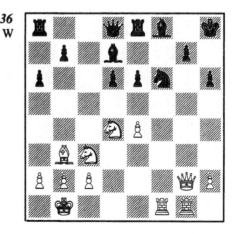

Solutions to Test 17

129. Vinkel–Gusev, Ashkhabad, 1964.
  1 R×d7! R×d7 (or *1 ... Q×d7 2 Nf6+!*) 2 Ne7++ Kg7 3 Qg8+ Kf6 4 Nd5 mate.

130. Perez–Garcia, Spain, 1957.
  1 R×d6!! R×d6 2 B×h7+! K×h7 (or *2 ... Kh8 3 Qh5!*) 3 Qh5+ Kg8 4 Ne7 mate.

131. Gaprindashvili–Veroczy, Belgrade, 1974 (variation).
  1 R×e5+!! f×e5 2 g4+ Kh4 3 Qe7+ Qg5 4 g3 mate. White missed this possibility, and after 1 Qg4+ Kh6 2 Qg7+ Kh5 3 Qg4+ the game ended in a draw.

132. David–Zeitan, Rumania, 1956.
  1 R1f6!! g×f6 (*1 ... Qh5 fails to 2 R×g7+! K×g7 3 Rg6+ Kh8 4 Qd2!!*) 2 Rh7! Qg5 3 Rh8+! Kf7 (*3 ... K×h8 4 Qh7 mate*) 4 Qh7+ Resigns (*4 ... Qg7 5 Bg6! mate*).

133. Rossolimo–Raizman, Puerto Rico, 1967.
  1 B×d5! c×d5 2 Nf6+ Kh8 3 Qg6!! Qc2 (*3 ... h×g6 4 Rh3 mate, or 3 ... f×g6 4 N×g6+ h×g6 5 Rh3 mate*) 4 Rh3! Resigns.

134. Duz–Khotimirsky v. Bannik, Vilnius, 1949.
  1 R×d4!! c×d4 (if *1 ... R×d5, then 2 R×d5 Q×d5 3 Nh6+*) 2 Nf6+! Kf8 (or *2 ... g×f6 3 Qh6!*) 3 Q×h7 g×f6 4 Re1 Resigns.

135. Dolmadzhyan–Angelov, Sofia, 1977.
  1 R×e7! R×e7 2 Nd6+! Kb8 (*2 ... Q×d6 3 R×e7 Q×e7 4 Qc6+*) 3 R×e7! Q×a4 4 Nb5+ Rd6 (otherwise mate) 5 B×d6+ Kc8 6 b3! Resigns (since if *6 ... Q×a2 7 Na7+ Kd8 8 Nc6+ Kc8 9 Rc7 mate*).

136. Spassky–Petrosian, Moscow, 1969.
  1 e5! d×e5 2 Ne4! Nh5 (*2 ... N×e4 3 R×f8+!*) 3 Qg6! e×d4 4 Ng5! Resigns (*4 ... h×g5 is met by 5 Q×h5+ Kg8 6 Qf7+ Kh8 7 Rf3!*).

Test 18   Positions 137–144

Theme: 'Square-vacation'. Seventy-five minutes are allowed for this test.

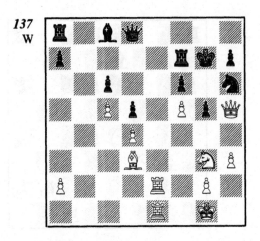

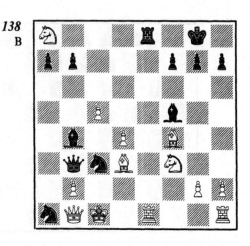

139
B

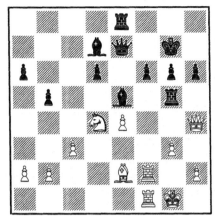

140
B

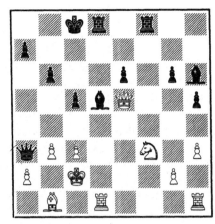

141
B

142
W

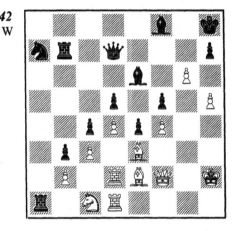

143
W

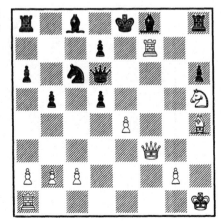

144
W

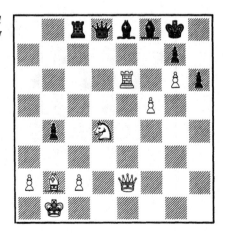

Solutions to Test 18

137. Van den Enden–Praszak, Lublin, 1974.
  1 Re8! Qc7 2 Q×g5+!! f×g5 3 Nh5 mate.
138. Druganov–Panteleyev, Corr., 1955/56.
  1 ... Qd1+!! 2 R×d1 Ne2+! 3 B×e2 Nb3 mate.
139. Radovici–Kolarov, Ploesti, 1957.
  1 ... Rh5!! 2 B×h5 g5! 3 B×e8 Q×e8 4 Q×h6+ K×h6 White resigns.
140. Bulakh–Petrov, Moscow, 1951.
  1 ... R×f3!! 2 g×f3 B×b3+! 3 a×b3 Qc1+! 4 R×c1 Rd2 mate.
141. Gurgenidze–Sergiyevsky, Novgorod, 1962.
  1 ... Bd2!! 2 Q×d2 N×e4 3 Qe3 Qg5+! 4 Q×g5 N×g5+, and Black won. There followed 5 Kg3 Rh3+ 6 Kg4 Bf3+ 7 Kg5, and White resigned.
142. Lobanov–Savilov, Frunze, 1967.
  1 B×c4!! d×c4 2 d5! Bg8 3 Bd4+ Bg7 4 h6! Qe8 5 h×g7+ R×g7 6 B×g7+ Resigns.
143. Mosionzhik–Listengarten, Minsk, 1963.
  1 Ng7+!! B×g7 2 Qh5!! Ne5 3 Rf6+ Ke7 4 Re6++! K×e6 5 Qf5 mate.
144. Vasyukov–Durasevic, Lvov, 1962.
  1 f6! g×f6 (or *1 ... B×g6 2 f×g7, and wins*) 2 g7! B×g7 3 Nf5 Bf8 4 Qg4+ Kh7 5 Re7+! Resigns.

Test 19   Positions 145–152

Theme: 'Line-opening'. In addition to this test, we devote to this theme two further tests, of increasing difficulty. This one is set for 65 minutes.

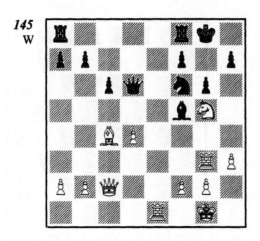

145
W

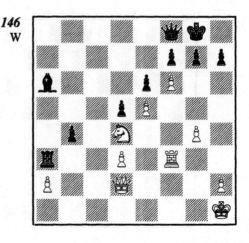

146
W

147
W

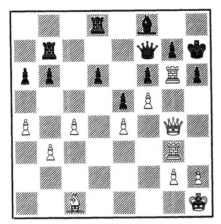

148
W

149
W

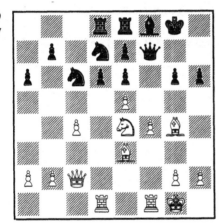

150
B

151
B

152
W

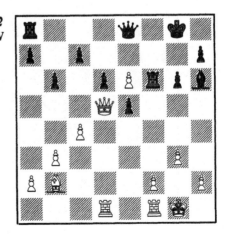

Solutions to Test 19

145. Kholmov–Golz, Dresden, 1956.
    1 Q×f5!! g×f5 2 Ne4+ Q×g3 3 N×f6+ Resigns (*3 ... Kg7 4 Nh5+*).

146. Westerinen–Diesen, Las Vegas, 1974.
    1 N×e6!! f×e6 2 f7+ Q×f7 (or *2 ... Kh8 3 Q×b4!!*) 3 R×f7, and White won. The game concluded 3 ... K×f7 4 Qf4+ Ke8 5 Q×b4 R×a2 6 Qb8+ Kd7 7 Qd6+ Kc8 8 Q×e6+ Kb8 9 Qb6+ Bb7 10 d4! Re2 11 Qd6+ Ka7 12 e6 Bc8 13 Qc7+, and Black resigned.

147. Nikolau–Iovanovic, Pernik, 1972.
    1 B×h6!! g×h6 2 R×f6! Bg7 (or *2 ... Qg7 3 R×h6+!*) 3 R×f7 Resigns.

148. Szabo–Stahlberg, Leipzig, 1960.
    1 Bd4!! N×d5 (or *1 ... e×d4 2 R×f4*) 2 R×e5! N×c3 (*3 Rh5!* was threatened) 3 B×c3 Resigns.

149. Szabo–Hemasian, Varna, 1962.
    1 Ng5!! h×g5 2 f×g5 Q×f1+ 3 R×f1 N×e5 4 B×e6+ Resigns.

150. Peterson–Ortiz, Corr., 1973.
    1 ... N×c2+ 2 Kf1 Rd1+! 3 B×d1 Ng3+! 4 f×g3 Qe1 mate.

151. Vuckevic–Panteleyev, Sofia, 1958.
    1 ... R×h2+!! 2 K×h2 Qf2+ 3 Kh3 Rh8+ 4 Kg4 Qf4 mate.

152. Jakobsen–Peterson, Copenhagen, 1968.
    1 e7+! Kh8 (*1 ... Kg7* is answered in the same way) 2 B×e5! d×e5 3 Q×a8+! Q×a8 4 Rd8 Resigns.

Test 20   Positions 153–160

Solving time—70 minutes.

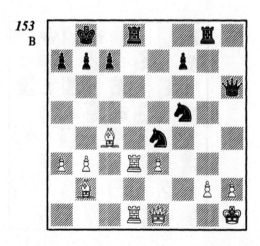

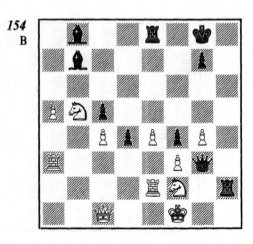

155
W

156
W

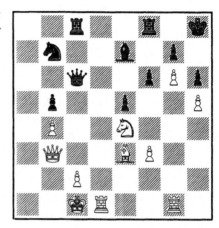

157
W

158
W

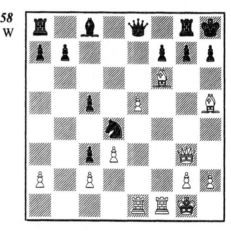

159
B

160
B

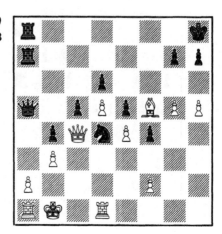

TYC—D

Solutions to Test 20

153. Kamishev–Estrin, Leningrad, 1951.
 1 ... Nfg3+ 2 Kg1 Q×h2+!! 3 K×h2 Rh8+ 4 B×h8 R×h8+ 5 Kg1 Rh1 mate.
154. A. Zaitsev–Gipslis, Moscow, 1969.
 1 ... B×e4! 2 Qd1 (*2 f×e4 f3!*) 2 ... Bd3!! 3 Q×d3 Qg2+ 4 Ke1 Q×f2+ White resigns.
155. Petkevich–Mosionzhik, Riga, 1964.
 1 B×g5!! f×g5 2 Q×g5+ Kh7 3 f6!! Qg6 4 Bg8+!! Resigns (*4 ... Q×g8 5 Qh5* mate).
156. Adorjan–Ostojic, Polanica Zdroj, 1970.
 1 B×h6! B×b4 2 B×g7+! K×g7 3 h6+! K×h6 4 g7 Rg8 5 Rg2! Resigns.
157. Berkkwist–Timman, Corr., 1971/72.
 1 Nh5!! g×h5 2 Ne6!! f×e6 3 Rg5+ Kf7 4 Qg6 mate.
158. Sax–Ciocaltea, Vrnjacka Banja, 1974.
 1 e6! B×e6 (on *1 ... N×e6* there follows *2 B×c3*, when Black is defenceless) 2 B×d4 c×d4 3 B×f7 Q×f7 4 R×f7, and White won. The finish was 4 ... B×f7 5 Qf4 B×a2 6 Q×d4, and Black resigned.
159. Grigorian–Balashov, Leningrad, 1974.
 1 ... N×e4! 2 f×e4 Q×g4+ 3 Rg2 (or *3 Kh2 Qh3+ 4 Kg1 Rf1* mate) 3 ... Rf1+ 4 Kh2 Qh3 mate.
160. Bublik–Kadaner, Izhevsk, 1974.
 1 ... Q×a2+!! 2 R×a2 R×a2 3 R×d4 (if *3 Kc1*, then *3 ... Ra1+ 4 Kd2 R8a2+ 5 Ke1 Nf3+ 6 Kf1 R×d1+ 7 Kg2 Nh4+ 8 Kh3 Rh1+ 9 Kg4 R×f2*, with inevitable mate) 3 ... Ra1+ 4 Kc2 R8a2+ White resigns (*5 Kd3 Rd1* mate).

Test 21   Positions 161–168

The concluding test on the theme of 'Line-opening'. Solving time—75 minutes.

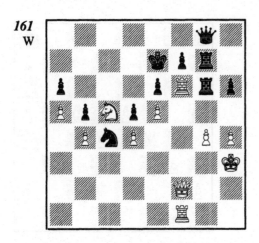

161
W

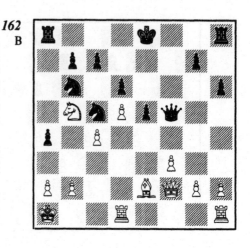

162
B

163
W

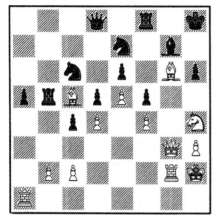

164
B

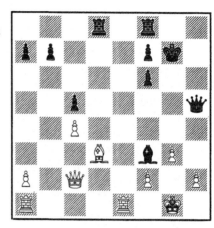

165
W

166
W

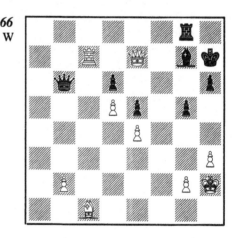

167
B

168
B

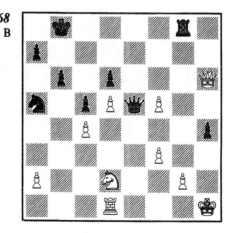

Solutions to Test 21

161. Pietzsch–Czerniak, Leipzig, 1960.
    1 N×e6!! f×e6 2 Rf8 Qh7 3 Ra8 Kd7 4 Qf8! Resigns.
162. Roizman–Sorokin, Odessa, 1952.
    1 ... Nb3+! 2 a×b3 a×b3+ 3 Na3 R×a3+! 4 b×a3 Qc2! White resigns.
163. Medina–Slisser, Amsterdam, 1967.
    1 Be8!! Rg8 2 B×c6 N×c6 3 Ng6+ Kh7 4 Nf8+! Kh8 5 Qg6!! Resigns.
164. Sobol–Garifulin, Corr., 1970.
    1 ... Qh3! (the immediate *1 ... Q×h2+* does not work on account of *2 K×h2 Rh8+ 3 Bh7!! R×h7 4 Q×h7+*) 2 Bf1 Q×h2+!! 3 K×h2 Rh8+ 4 Bh3 R×h3+! 5 K×h3 Rh8+ White resigns.
165. Veresov–Bunatian, Moscow, 1965.
    1 N×d5!! e×d5 (*1 ... f×e5 is met by 2 Ne7+ Kh8 3 Qh4!*, and *1 ... f×g5 by 2 Ne7+ Kh8 3 Q×f8+ B×f8 4 N×g6+ and 5 R×a5*) 2 R×d5 Qb6 (*2 ... Q×d5 3 Bc4!*) 3 Qc4 Be6 4 Be3! Resigns. After 4 ... Q×b2, 5 Bd4 is decisive, while on 4 ... Qc6 White wins by 5 Q×c6 b×c6 6 Rd6 Bd5 7 c4.
166. Evans–Uhlmann, Amsterdam, 1971.
    1 B×g5! h×g5 2 Qf7 Kh6 3 Re7 Resigns (against the threat of *4 Re6+* there is no defence).
167. Ivkov–Garcia, Tel Aviv, 1964.
    1 ... Nh4+!! 2 g×h4 Qg4+ 3 Kf1 Qh3+ 4 Qg2 Qd3+ White resigns.
168. Mohring–Fuchs, East Germany, 1972.
    1 ... Qg3! 2 Rg1 h3! 3 Q×h3 Qg7!, and Black wins (e.g. *4 Ne4 Rh8 5 f6 Qf8*).

Test 22   Positions 169–176

The theme 'Utilization of open files' is almost a continuation of the previous theme. Time for the solving of these positions—60 minutes.

169
W

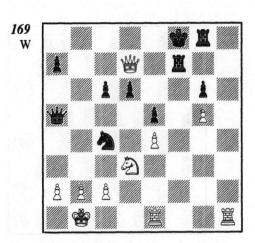

170
W

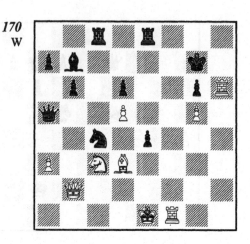

171
W

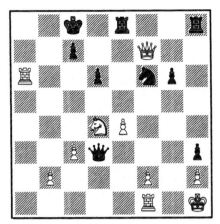

172
B

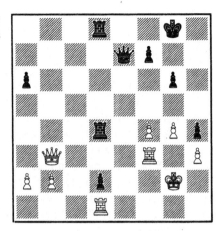

173
W

174
B

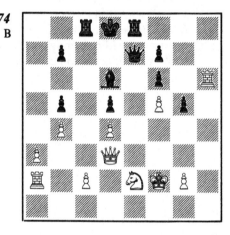

175
B

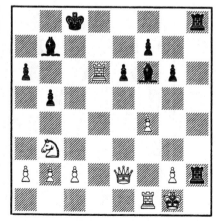

176
W

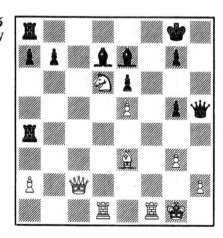

Solutions to Test 22

169. Grunke–Muller, Corr., 1963.
     1 Qc8+! Kg7 2 Rh7+!! K×h7 3 Qh3+ Kg7 4 Qh6 mate.
170. Nrashkin–Nikhayev, Corr., 1965.
     1 Rf7+! Kg8 (if *1 ... K×f7*, then *2 Qf2+ and mates*) 2 Rh8+!! K×h8 3 Qh2+ Kg8 3 Qh7 mate.
171. Berkit–Fritzinger, California, 1969 (variation).
     1 Ra8+! Kb7 2 Qb3+ K×a8 3 Ra1+ Qa6 4 R×a6 mate. The game in fact went 1 Rfa1 Q×e4+ 2 f3 Qe1+ 3 R×e1 R×e1 mate.
172. Stahlberg–Szabo, Neuhausen, 1953.
     1 ... Rd3!! 2 R×d3 Qe2+ 3 Kg1 R×d3 4 Qb8+ Kh7 White resigns.
173. Tal–Wade, Palma de Mallorca, 1966.
     1 R×h7!! N×h7 2 Qh6 e6 3 f4! e5 4 g5! Be8 5 Ne6!! Resigns (on *5 ... f×e6* there comes *6 Q×h7+ Kf8 7 Qh8+ Ke7 8 Rh7+ Bf7 9 Q×c8*).
174. Ostojic–Marangunic, Yugoslavia, 1969.
     1 ... Rc3!! 2 Qd2 Re3! 3 c3 g4 4 Rh5 Qe4! White resigns.
175. Kostro–Schmidt, Polanica Zdroj, 1968.
     1 ... Bh4!! 2 Rd8+ (there is no adequate defence against the threat of *2 ... Rh1+! 3 K×h1 Bf2+*) 2 ... B×d8 3 Nd4 Bb6 4 c3 R×g2+, and Black won.
176. Karasev–Tseitlin, Leningrad, 1975.
     1 Nf5 Qe8 (Black also fails to save the game after *1 ... e×f5 2 R×d7 Re4 3 R×e7—3 Qb3+ is weaker in view of 3 ... Qf7!—3 ... R×e3 4 Q×f5 Re2 5 Qf7+ Q×f7 6 Rf×f7 R×a2 7 R×g7+ Kf8 8 R×b7, and wins*) 2 R×d7 Q×d7 3 N×e7+ Kh8 4 Rf7!! Resigns (*4 ... Qe8 5 Qg6!, or 4 ... Qd8 5 Q×a4*).

Test 23   Positions 177–184

We conclude the theme 'Utilization of open files' (Nos. 177–180) and begin 'Diagonal-opening' (Nos. 181–184). The time for this test is 60 minutes.

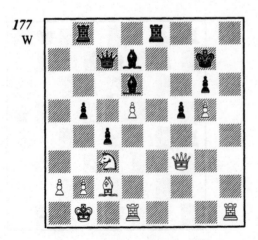

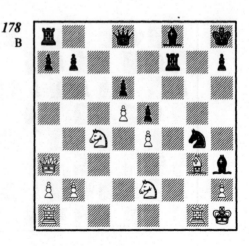

181
W

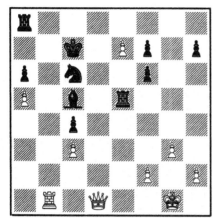

180
W

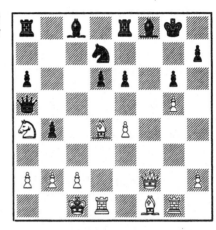

181
W

182
W

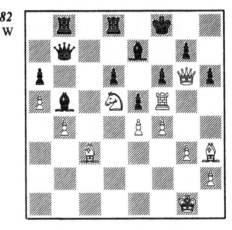

183
W

184
W

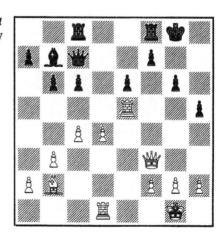

Solutions to Test 23

177. Kozlovskaya–J. Hartston, Minorca, 1973.
 1 Ne4! Be5 2 Nf6! B×f6 3 g×f6+ K×f6 4 Rh7! Rbd8 5 Qf2! Resigns.

178. Lerch–Castanga, Switzerland, 1973.
 1 ... Rf2!! 2 Rge1 (if *2 B×f2 N×f2 mate*, while *2 ... R×h2+ 3 B×h2 Nf2 mate* was also threatened) 2 ... Qg5 3 Rad1 R×h2+! 4 Kg1 (or *4 B×h2 Nf2 mate*) 4 ... Rg2+ 5 Kh1 Nf2+! 6 B×f2 Rh2+! White resigns (*7 K×h2 Qg2 mate*).

179. Tal–Keller, Zurich, 1959.
 1 Rb7+! K×b7 2 Qd7+ Kb8 3 e8=Q+ R×e8 4 Q×e8+ Kb7 5 Qd7+ Kb8 6 Q×c6 Resigns.

180. Espig–Adamski, Lublin, 1970.
 1 Bc4!! Q×a4 2 Rgf1 Ne5 3 B×e5 d×e5 4 Qf7+ Kh8 5 Rd8!! Bb7 6 Rd7! Resigns.

181. Hort–Portisch, Madrid, 1973.
 1 Rg4+!! f×g4 2 Qg5+ Kh8 3 Qh6! Resigns.

182. Avirovich–Tagirov, Corr., 1948.
 1 Rg5!! f×g5 2 Be6 Be8 3 Qh7! Resigns.

183. Meyer–Petral, Corr., 1954/56.
 1 d6! Q×d6 2 Qc4+ Kh7 3 Qf7+ Resigns.

184. Larsson–Andersson, Göteborg, 1971.
 1 d5! c×d5 (no better is *1 ... Qd8 2 Qc3!*) 2 Qf6 Qd8 3 Qh8+!! Resigns (*3 ... K×h8 4 R×h5++ Kg8 5 Rh8 mate*).

Test 24   Positions 185–192

Continuation of the theme 'Diagonal-opening'. Time allowed—55 minutes.

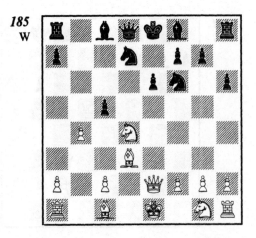

185
W

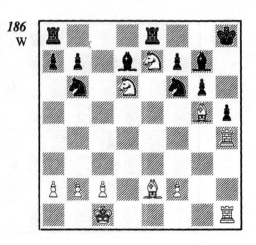

186
W

187
B

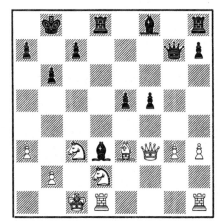

188
W

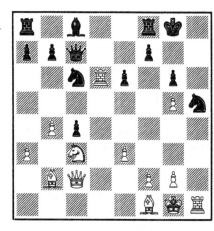

189
W

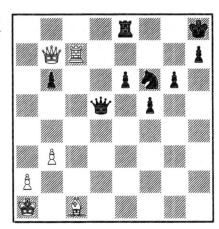

190
B

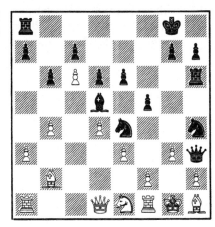

191
B

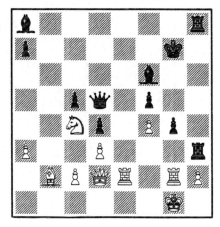

192
W

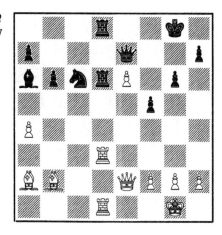

Solutions to Test 24

185. Perenyi–Eperjessy, Budapest, 1974.
     1 Nc6! Qc7 2 Q×e6+!! f×e6 3 Bg6 mate.
186. Kosikov–Kalinsky, Kharkov, 1974.
     1 R×h5+!! g×h5 2 R×h5+ N×h5 (or *2 ... Bh6 3 B×f6+*) 3 N×f7+ Kh7 4 Bd3+
     Resigns.
187. Liberman–Simenau, Bucharest, 1950.
     1 ... e4! 2 Q×f5 (other continuations are no better) 2 ... Q×c3+!! 3 b×c3 B×a3 mate.
188. Benaru–Hartlaub, Munich, 1949.
     1 R×h5!! g×h5 2 Nd5!! e×d5 3 Qh7+! Resigns. After 3 ... K×h7 there follows 4 Rh6+
     Kg8 Rh8 mate.
189. Arinbjorn–Gundmunder, Reykjavik, 1958.
     1 R×h7+!! N×h7 2 Bb2+ e5 3 Q×d5 Resigns.
190. Mulberg–Fuchs, Berlin, 1965.
     1 ... Nd2! 2 Q×d2 Q×h2+!! 3 K×h2 Nf3++ White resigns (*4 Kg2 Rh2* is mate).
191. Diekstra–Kaizer, Beverwijk, 1951.
     1 ... R×h2! 2 R×h2 Qh1+!! 3 R×h1 R×h1+ 4 Kf2 Bh4 mate.
192. Uhlmann–Darga, Hastings, 1958/59.
     1 R×d6! R×d6 (or *1 ... B×e2 2 R×d8+ N×d8 3 R×d8+ Q×d8 4 e7+*) 2 R×d6!
     Resigns. On 2 ... B×e2 there can follow 3 Bf6!! Q×f6 4 e7+ Kg7 5 e8=N+!!

Test 25   Positions 193–200

This further test on the theme 'Diagonal-opening' is rather more difficult than the previous
one. The solving time allowed is 65 minutes.

193
B

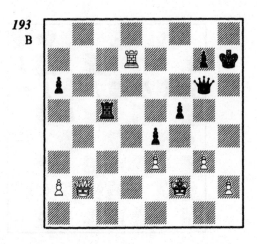

194
W

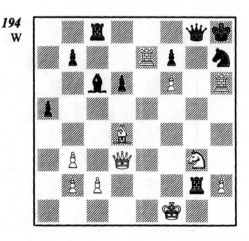

195
W

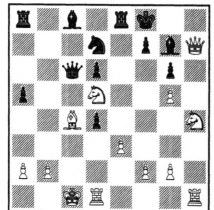

196
W

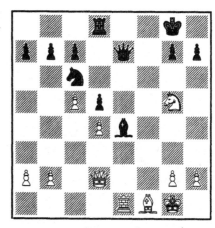

197
W

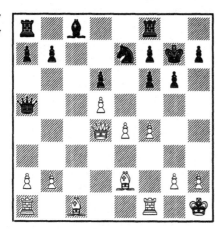

198
W

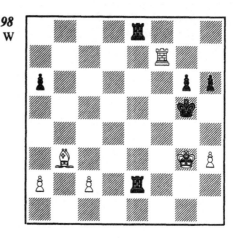

199
B

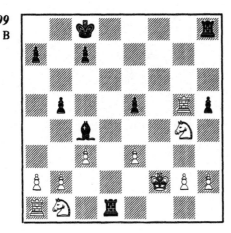

200
W

Solutions to Test 25

193. A. Zaitsev–Szabo, Ludwigsburg, 1969.
    1 ... f4! 2 e×f4 (the threat of *2 ... f×g3+* followed by *3 ... Rf5+* was very strong)
    2 ... Rc2+!! 3 Q×c2 e3+ White resigns.
194. Mosionzhik–Gornyak, Kishinev, 1969.
    1 R×f7! Q×f7 2 Q×h7+! Q×h7 3 f7 mate.
195. Jerstrom–Bergman, Lusdal, 1950.
    1 N×g6+!! f×g6 2 Qg8+!! K×g8 3 Ne7++ Kf8 4 N×g6 mate.
196. Tikhanov–Shmelev, Moscow, 1970.
    1 R×e4!! d×e4 2 Bc4+ Kf8 3 Qf4+ Ke8 4 Bf7+ Resigns.
197. Vanka–Skala, Prague, 1960.
    1 b4!! Qd8 2 Q×f6+! K×f6 3 Bb2 mate.
198. Malmberg–Nordstrem, Stockholm, 1964.
    1 h4+! Kh5 2 Rf5+!! g×f5 3 Bf7 mate.
199. Georgiev–Kadrev, Sofia, 1965.
    1 ... Rf1+!! 2 Kg3 h4+ 3 Kh3 Rf3+!! 4 g×f3 Bf1 mate.
200. Kwinetzki–Kedzigra, Poznan, 1952.
    1 N×e5!! R×e5 2 Rf6! Qc7 3 Qe7!! R×e7 (no better is *3 ... Re8 4 Rf8+ R×f8 5 Q×f8 mate*) 4 Rf8 mate.

Test 26   Positions 201–208

We conclude 'Diagonal-opening' (Nos. 201–204) and also give four examples (Nos. 205–208) on a directly-related theme 'Utilization of open diagonals'. The positions are quite difficult, and therefore 75 minutes are allowed for this test.

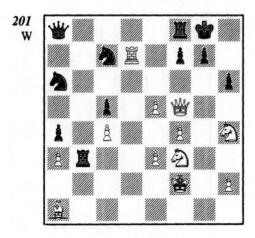

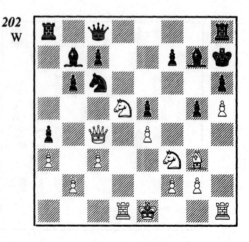

203
B

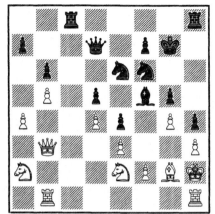

204
B

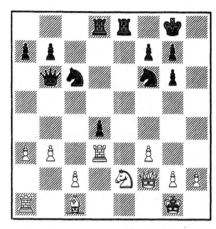

205
W

206
B

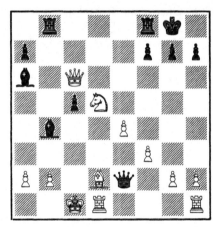

207
B

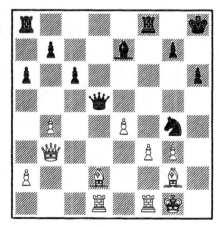

208
B

Solutions to Test 26

201. Grinszpan–Kaminski, Poznan, 1961.
  1 Ng5!! h×g5 2 Ng6!! f×g6 (forced, since *3 Ne7+ Kh8 4 Qh3* mate was threatened) 3 R×g7+!! K×g7 4 e6+ Resigns.

202. Ljubojcvic–Padevsky, Nice, 1974.
  1 Nf6+! B×f6 2 Q×f7+ Bg7 3 N×g5+! h×g5 4 h6 Resigns.

203. Kamshonkov–Terentiev, Sverdlovsk, 1974.
  1 ... B×g4!! 2 h×g4 h3 3 B×h3 (on *3 Bf1* there follows *3 ... N×g4+ 4 Kg1 h2+*) 3 ... R×h3+! 4 K×h3 N×d4!! White resigns.

204. Kabadziyan–Chikhelashvili, Tbilisi, 1974.
  1 ... Ne5! 2 R×d4 (on *2 Rd1* there follows *2 ... Neg4! 3 f×g4 N×g4 4 Qf4 d3+*) 2 ... Neg4! 3 f×g4 N×g4 4 Qf4 R×d4!! White resigns (on *5 Q×d4* comes *5 ... Q×d4 6 N×d4 Re1* mate).

205. Jagodzinski–Kupinski, Poznan, 1974.
  With his last move ... g5 Black chose an untimely moment to play actively, and this is what happened: 1 Re8+!! Kg7 (after *1 ... Q×e8 2 Q×f6* White mates) 2 Ne6+! Kh6 (*2 ... B×e6 3 Q×g5+!*) 3 N×d8 g×f4 4 B×f6 Nd7 5 Rg8 Resigns.

206. Gheorghiu–Rossolimo, Beverwijk, 1968 (variation).
  1 ... Bb5! 2 Qc7 Bd3!! 3 Nf4 Ba3! 4 Qe5 R×b2! 5 Q×b2 Rb8! and wins. Black in fact played 1 ... Bd3 immediately, overlooking the reply 2 Qa4, and the game ended in a draw.

207. Gutman–Tseshkovsky, Lvov, 1973.
  1 ... Bc5+! 2 b×c5 Q×c5+ 3 Be3 Q×e3+ 4 Q×e3 N×e3 5 Rd7 N×f1 6 K×f1 b5, and Black won.

208. Airapetov–Pavlenko, Sumgait, 1972.
  1 ... R×f4+! 2 g×f4 R×g1 3 K×g1 Qh1+ 4 Kf2 Bh4+ 5 Ke3 Qc1+! 6 Qd2 Qg1+ White resigns.

Test 27 Positions 209–216

Eight examples on the theme of 'Smothered mate'. Fifty minutes are allowed for this test, which should not cause you too much difficulty.

209
W

210
B

White played 1 Bf4, thinking that by this move he had defended his knight at d6. But Black assumed that, on account of the pin on the d-file, he would not only regain his piece, but also obtain good attacking chances. Who was right?

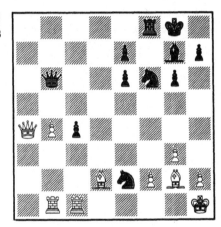

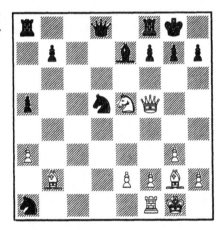

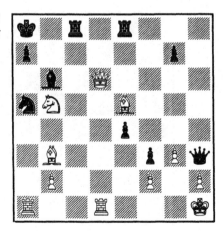

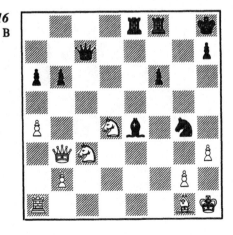

Solutions to Test 27

209. Unzicker–Sarapu, Siegen, 1970.
     1 Bf4! N×f4 2 Q×f7+ Kh8 3 Qg8+!! R×g8 4 Nf7 mate.
210. Sif–Kashdan, New York, 1948.
     1 ... Nhg3+ 2 Kh2 Nf1++ 3 Kh1 Qh2+!! 4 N×h2 Nfg3 mate.
211. Mayevskaya–Kirienko, Zhitomir, 1974.
     1 Qh7+!! N×h7 2 Nhg6+ Kg8 3 N×e7+ Kh8 4 N5g6 mate.
212. Najdorf–N.N., Rafaela, 1947 (from a simultaneous display).
     1 Qh5! B×d5 2 R×d5!! Q×d5 3 Q×f7+!! Q×f7 4 Nd7 mate.
213. Stashkov–Klimenko, Zhitomir, 1973.
     1 ... Ng4! 2 Be1 (or *2 Be3 Q×e3!*) 2 ... Q×f2!! 3 Bd2 Qg1+! 4 R×g1 Nf2 mate.
214. Benko–Horwitz, New York, 1968.
     1 N×f7! Qc8 (or *1 ... R×f7 2 B×d5 and wins*) 2 Nh6+ Kh8 3 Q×d5 Nc2 4 Qg8+!!
     Resigns.
215. Ferarini–Morezi, Verona, 1972.
     1 Bd5+ Nb7 2 Qb8+! R×b8 3 R×a7+! B×a7 4 Nc7 mate.
216. Poutiainen–Szabo, Budapest, 1975.
     1 ... B×g2+! 2 K×g2 Rg8! 3 Kh1 (*3 h×g4 R×g4+ 4 Kf1 Qg3 5 Nce2 Qg2+ 6 Ke1*
     Q×g1+ 7 Kd2 Q×a1 and wins) 3 ... Qh2+!! White resigns (*4 B×h2 Nf2 mate*).

Test 28   Positions 217–224

Two themes are covered in this test: 'Blocking' (Nos. 217–222) and 'X-ray' or 'The penetrating action of pieces' (Nos. 223 and 224). Some of the examples are not easy, and so the time allowed is 70 minutes.

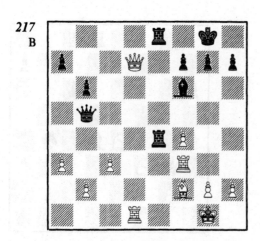

217
B

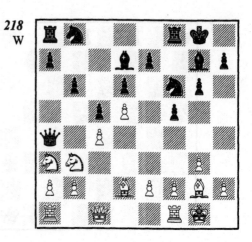

218
W

219
W

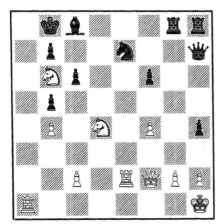

220
B

221
W

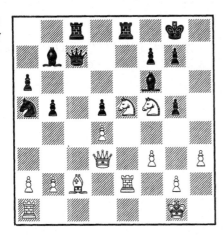

222
W

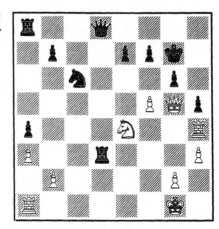

223
W

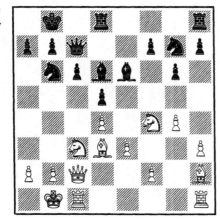

224
B

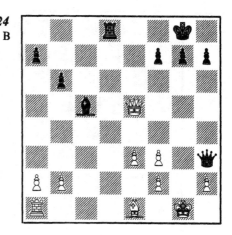

Solutions to Test 28

217. Kuzmichev–Shereshevsky, Daugavpils, 1973.
     1 ... Re1+! 2 B×e1 R×e1+ 3 Kf2 Bh4+!! and mate next move.
218. Minev–Ioakimidis, Sofia, 1979.
     1 Na5! Resigns (the queen is lost after *1 ... b×a5 2 b3*, or *1 ... Be8 2 Nb5!*).
219. Euwe–Rossetto, Buenos Aires, 1947.
     1 N×b5!! c×b5 2 Qc5! Nc6 3 Qd6+ Qc7 4 Ra8 mate.
220. Evans–Karaklajic, Italy, 1962.
     1 ... Q×g5+!! 2 Q×g5 B×g5+ 3 K×g5 h4! White resigns (against *4 ... Rh5* mate there is no defence).
221. Garcia–Wasserstrom, Buenos Aires, 1968.
     1 Ne7+!! Kf8 (if *1 ... R×e7*, then *2 Qh7+ Kf8 3 Qh8* mate) 2 Nd7+! Q×d7 3 Qh7! Resigns.
222. Ortega–Brink, Varna, 1962.
     1 R×h5! Qd4+ 2 Kh2 Qe5+ 3 Kh1 Q×e4 4 f6+!! Resigns.
223. Reshevsky–Gligoric, New York, 1952.
     1 Nb5!! c×b5 2 Q×c7+ B×c7 3 R×c7 K×c7 4 N×e6++ Kd7 5 N×d8 R×d8 6 B×b5+, and White won.
224. Szabadi–Pogats, Budapest, 1963.
     1 ... Bd6! 2 Rd1 (*2 Qe4* is strongly met by *2 ... B×h2+ 3 Kh1 h5!*, with the threat of ... *Rd6–g6*) 2 ... Q×h2+!! 3 Q×h2 B×h2+ 3 K×h2 R×d1 White resigns.

Test 29   Positions 225–232

Theme: 'Combinations based on the overloading of pieces'. The test is set for 60 minutes.

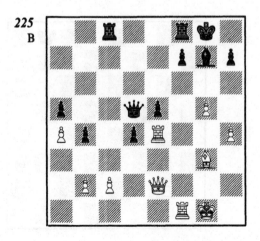

225
B

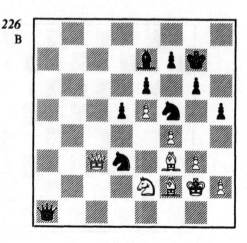

226
B

227
W

228
W

229
W

230
B

231
B

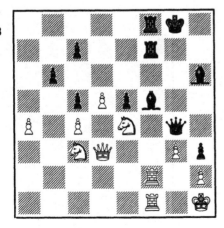

232
W

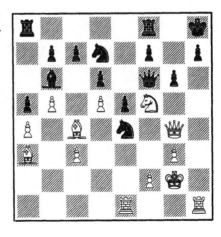

Solutions to Test 29

225. Ilievsky–Gulko, Moscow, 1973.
     1 ... b3! 2 c×b3 d3 3 Rd1 Rc1!! White resigns.
226. Chuit–Podgayets, Leningrad, 1974.
     1 ... Nh4+!! 2 g×h4 N×f4+ 3 Kg3 N×e2+ White resigns (*4 B×e2 Q×c3+*).
227. Klundt–Gerer, Corr., 1970.
     1 N×d5! e×d5 2 N×d7 Q×d7 3 B×h7+! Resigns (*3 ... N×h7 4 Q×d7 or 3 ... Kh8 4 Bf5+!*).
228. Duckstein–Fichtl, Prague, 1957.
     1 Rc1 Qa4 2 Q×e4!! Q×e4 3 Ne7+!! Resigns (*3 ... R×e7 4 Rc8+*).
229. K. Richter–Weschtzig, Hemnitz, 1948.
     1 Nf8!! R×d3 (or *1 ... g6 2 N×g6+ h×g6 3 h×g6+*) 2 Ng6+!! h×g6 3 h×g6+ Qh7 4 R×h7+ Resigns.
230. Raaste–Sax, Nice, 1974.
     1 ... Qh5!! 2 Q×f3 Q×f3 3 R×f3 R×c1+ 4 B×c1 R×f3 White resigns.
231. Trubnikov–Radchenko, Novorossisk, 1965.
     1 ... Bd2! 2 Q×d2 (if *2 R×f5, then 2 ... R×f5 3 N×d2 R×f1+ 4 N×f1 e4 5 N×e4 Q×e4+*) 2 ... B×e4+ 3 Kg1 (or *3 N×e4 Q×e4+ 4 Kg1 Qg2+!!*) 3 ... Q×g3+!! 4 h×g3 h2+! White resigns (*5 K×h2 Rh7+ 6 Kg1 Rh1 mate*).
232. Berczy–Tompa, Budapest, 1965.
     1 R×h7+!! K×h7 2 Rh1+ Kg8 3 Qh3 Ng5 4 Ne7+! Resigns.

Test 30   Positions 233–240

The theme 'Exploiting a back rank weakness' is one to which we devoted a great deal of attention in Book 1. This test is set for 75 minutes.

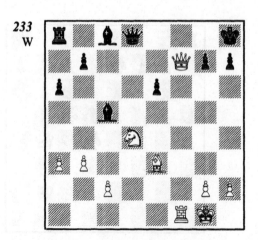

233
W

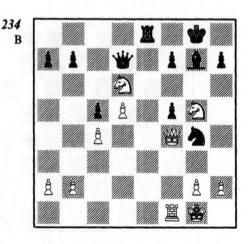

234
B

235
B

236
W

237
W

238
W

239
B

240
W

Solutions to Test 30

233. Honfi–Lengyel, Budapest, 1961.
     1 Nc6! b×c6 (or *1 ... B×e3+ 2 Kh1 Qg8 3 Q×g8+ K×g8 4 Ne7+ and wins*) 2 B×c5 Bd7 (*2 ... h6 3 Qg6!!*) 3 Bd4 Resigns (on *3 ... Qg8* there follows *4 Q×d7 Rd8 5 B×g7+!!*).

234. Brinck–Claussen v. Littlewood, Varna, 1962.
     1 ... Q×d6!! 2 Q×d6 Bd4+ 3 Kh1 Nf2+ White resigns (*4 R×f2 Re1+* or *4 Kg1 Ne4+*).

235. Ziegmund–Eret, Corr., 1951.
     1 ... N×g3!! 2 h×g3 (on *2 B×d5* there comes *2 ... Ne4+ 3 Kh1 N×f2+!! 4 R×f2 R×d1+*) 2 ... R×g3+!! 3 f×g3 Qg2 mate.

236. Ilivitsky–Sokolsky, Kiev, 1954.
     1 Q×e3!! R×e3 2 Nd5!! Qh6 (*2 ... Ne6 3 Ne7 mate, or 2 ... h6 3 Rf8+ and 4 Rh8 mate*) 3 Nf6+ Q×f6 (*any king move is answered by 4 Ng4+*) 4 R×f6 and White wins. The finish was 4 ... Re8 5 Rf7 Re5 6 Bh3 Bb6 7 Rf8+ Kg7 8 Be5+ Resigns.

237. Stephenson–Blaine, London, 1962.
     1 Rd8+!! Q×d8 2 Q×e5 Qd7 3 Qh8+!! K×h8 4 Rf8 mate.

238. Rovner–Kamishev, Moscow, 1946.
     1 Qa7!! Qa5 (if *1 ... Qc8 2 Q×b8!*, while on *1 ... Rdc8* there follows *2 Q×c7 R×c7 3 Rd8+ and mates*) 2 Q×a6! Qc7 3 Qa7! Resigns.

239. Schmid–Turner, Stuttgart, 1953.
     1 ... Bd3! 2 Ra1 Rc2 3 e4 (on *3 Qf4* there follows *3 ... R×a2 4 Q×f7+ Kh7 5 Rc1 Qd2!*) 3 ... R×a2 4 e5 Q×f2+! White resigns.

240. Zakharov–Dzhanoyev, Grozny, 1973.
     1 N×b5! g5 (if *1 ... N×b5, then 2 Qh6 Qf8 3 Ra8!*) 2 Q×e5!! d×e5 3 N×c7 Q×f6 4 Ra8+ Resigns (*4 ... Kg7 5 Ne8+*).

Test 31   Positions 241–248

Here there are four examples on the preceding theme (Nos. 241–244) and four on the theme 'Weakness of the second rank'. The time for this test is 60 minutes.

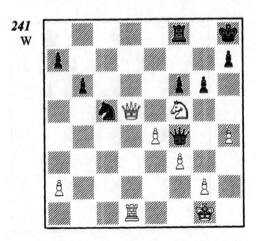

241
W

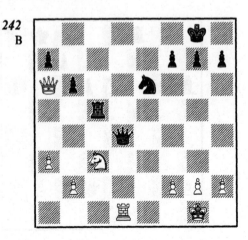

242
B

243
W

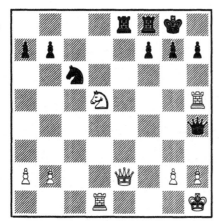

244
B

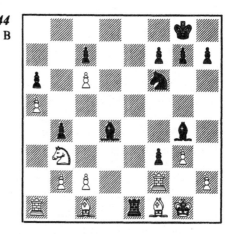

245
W

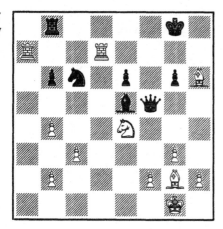

246
B

247
B

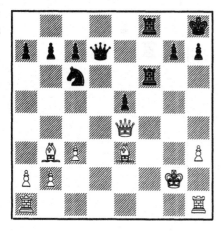

248
W

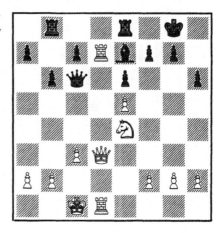

Solutions to Test 31

241. Vilert–O'Kelly, Brussels, 1952.
     1 Qf7!! Ne6 2 Rd8! Qc1+ (or *2 ... R×d8 3 Q×f6+ Kg8 4 Ne7 mate*) 3 Kh2 Qf4+ 4 Kh3 Resigns.
242. Polyak–Levin, Kiev, 1949.
     1 ... R×c3!! 2 Qf1 Rc8! 3 R×d4 N×d4 4 Kh1 Ne2!! White resigns.
243. Sampuf–Silalakhi, Indonesia, 1971.
     1 Q×e8!! Q×h5 2 Ne7+! N×e7 3 Q×f8+!! K×f8 4 Rd8 mate.
244. Madan–Grager, Tel Aviv, 1964.
     1 ... B×f2+ 2 K×f2 Ne4+!! 3 Kg1 (*3 K×e1 f2 mate*) 3 ... R×f1+! 4 K×f1 Bh3+ White resigns.
245. Stein–Sokolsky, Odessa, 1960.
     1 Rg7+! B×g7 (*1 ... Kh8 2 Rh7+ Kg8 3 Rag7+*) 2 R×g7+ Kh8 3 Rc7! Resigns. There is no defence against 4 Bg7+ Kg8 (or *4 ... Kh7*) 5 Nf6+.
246. Shestoperov–Guldin, Moscow, 1963.
     1 ... Nd4!! 2 R×c8 (or *2 Re5 Qf5 3 Rce1 Ne2+!!*) 2 ... Ne2+ 3 Kh1 N×g3+ 4 h×g3 Ra×c8, and Black won.
247. Steinsapir–Estrin, Moscow, 1946.
     1 ... Rg6+ 2 Kh2 Qd2+!! 3 B×d2 Rf2+ 4 Qg2 Rf×g2 mate.
248. Gusev–Veltmander, Gorky, 1955.
     1 R×e7!! R×e7 2 Nf6+! Kf8 (or *2 ... g×f6 3 e×f6 Q×g2 4 f×e7 Qg5+ 5 Qe3 Q×e7 6 Q×h6*) 3 Qh7! Ree8 4 Rd7! Resigns.

Test 32   Positions 249–256

The theme of this test is 'Intermediate move' or 'Zwischenzug'. In each example you are set a specific problem. The solving time allowed is 60 minutes.

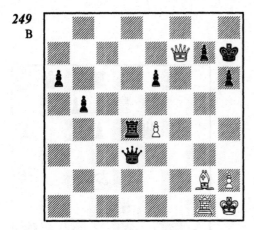

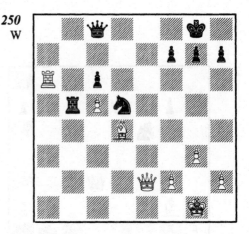

Black played 1 ... R×e4, thinking that after 2 B×e4+ Q×e4+ the game would end in a draw, but ... this is not what happened. What did he miss?

After 1 Qg4 Black resigned, but later it was found that this was a premature decision. What is the point?

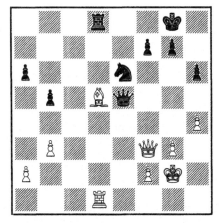

251
B

In order to make ... Nd4 possible, Black played 1 ... Kh8, thinking that after 2 B×e6 R×d1 3 Q×d1 Q×e6 he would be able to draw. But is this so?

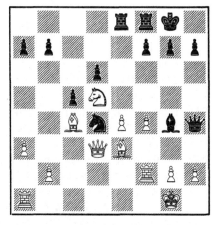

252
B

It appears that White has missed 1 ... R×e4, and if Q×e4 Bf5. But is this so?

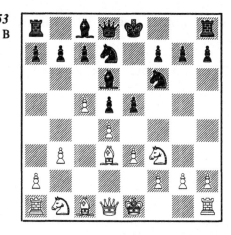

253
B

Black went in for this position, thinking that after 1 ... B×c5 2 d×c5 e4 he would not only regain his piece, but also gain the better position. Where did he go wrong?

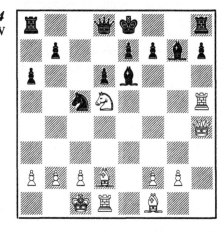

254
W

Both players happily went in for this position. Black thought that after 1 Ba5 he had a satisfactory defence. Is this so?

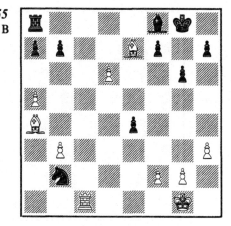

255
B

Black saw that after 1 ... B×e7 2 d×e7 N×a4 3 Rd1! White wins, and so he chose 1 ... N×a4. But here too an unpleasant surprise awaited him. What was it?

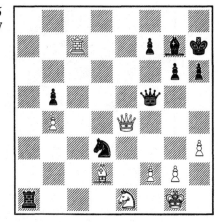

256
W

Wishing to simplify the position, White played 1 Q×f5, which met with an unpleasant reply. What was it?

Solutions to Test 32

249. Fleschman–Blume, Berlin, 1947.
 1 ... R×e4?? 2 Qg6+! K×g6 3 B×e4++ Resigns.
250. Engelburg–Hofmann, Leipzig, 1961.
 1 Qg4? Rb1+! 2 Kg2 Nf4+! 3 g×f4 (if *3 Q×f4 Q×a6*, or *3 Kf3 Ne6*) 3 ... Q×g4+, and
 Black wins.
251. Bilek–Farago, Budapest, 1974.
 1 ... Kh8? 2 B×e6! R×d1 3 Qa8+!! Resigns (on *3 ... Kh7* comes *4 B×f7!*, with inevitable
 mate).
252. Addison–Kostro, Havana, 1966.
 1 ... R×e4?? 2 Q×e4 Bf5 3 g3!! Resigns.
253. Najdorf–Donner, Amsterdam, 1950.
 1 ... B×c5?? 2 d×c5 e4 3 c6!! b×c6 (or *3 ... Nb6 4 Bb5!*) 4 Nd4 Resigns.
254. Krogius–Borisenko, Leningrad, 1953.
 1 Ba5! b6 2 B×b6! B×b2+ 3 Kb1 Rb8 (it was on this move that Black had based his
 hopes, but ...) 4 Bb5+!! Resigns.
255. Najdorf–Stahlberg, Buenos Aires, 1946.
 1 ... N×a4 2 d7!! (after *2 b×a4 f5* Black saves the game) 2 ... B×e7 3 Rc8+ Kg7 4 b×a4
 Resigns.
256. Barcza–Bronstein, Moscow, 1949.
 1 Q×f5? N×e1!! 2 Kf1 (forced, since if *2 Q×f7 Nf3* mate) 2 ... Nc2+ 3 Bc1 R×c1+ 4
 Ke2 Nd4+ 5 Kd2 Nb3+ White resigns.

Test 33   Positions 257–264

This test demonstrates instances, which occur very frequently in practical play, where a
passed pawn has to be utilized. It also instructs on the creation of passed pawns. The test is
set for 65 minutes.

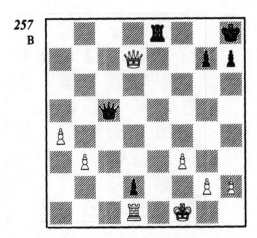

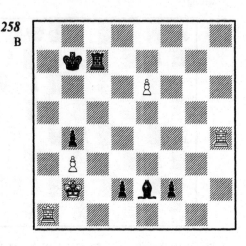

259
B

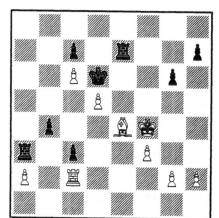

260
B

261
B

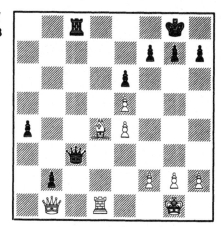

262
B

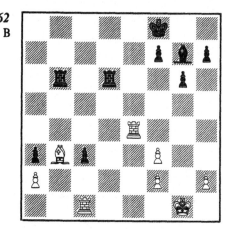

263
B

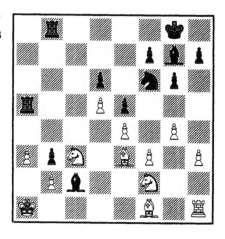

264
W

Solutions to Test 33

257. N.N.–Guimard, Bordeaux, 1966.
    1 ... Re1+! 2 R×e1 Qg1+!! 3 K×g1 d×e1=Q mate.
258. Murey–Belyavsky, Sukhumi, 1972.
    1 ... Rc2+!! 2 K×c2 d1=Q+ 3 R×d1 B×d1+ White resigns.
259. Hartman–Redish, Corr., 1954/56.
    1 ... R×a2!! 2 R×a2 R×e4+!! 3 K×e4 b3! White resigns.
260. Szalay–Marillay, Hungary, 1971 (variation).
    1 ... g3! 2 Nf3+ Kh5 3 N×d4 h2+! 4 Kg2 g×f2, and wins. Black in fact played 1 ... Bc5?, and after 2 N×g4! the game ended in a draw.
261. Sapi–Barczay, Budapest, 1963.
    1 ... Q×d4!! 2 R×d4 Rc1+ 3 Rf1 R×b1 4 R×b1 a3 White resigns.
262. Flohr–Tolush, Moscow, 1946.
    1 ... R×b3!! 2 a×b3 a2 3 Kg2 (or *3 Ra4 c2!*) 3 ... c2 4 R×c2 Bb2! White resigns.
263. Chepukaitis–Tseitlin, Leningrad, 1967.
    1 ... N×d5!! 2 e×d5 R×a3+! 3 b×a3 b2+ 4 Ka2 b1=Q+ White resigns.
264. Filip–Urbanek, Prague, 1955.
    1 Q×e8!! Q×e8 2 B×f7+! Q×f7 3 R×c8+ Qf8 4 d7! Resigns.

Test 34   Positions 265–272

The two themes in this test are 'Breakthrough' (Nos. 265–268) and 'Simplifying combinations' (Nos. 269–272). Eighty minutes are allowed for this test, which is more difficult than the preceding ones.

265
W

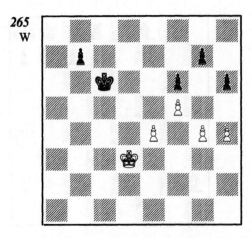

266
B

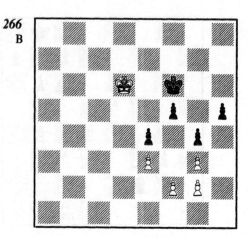

267
W

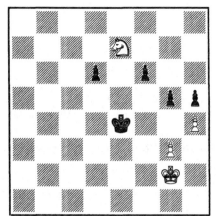

268
B

269
W

270
B

271
B

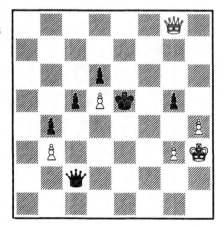

272
B

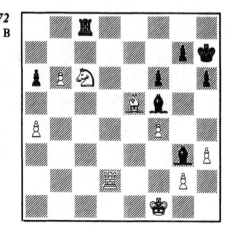

Solutions to Test 34

265. Averbakh–Bebchuk, Moscow, 1964.

1 e5!! f×e5 2 g5!! h×g5 (on *2 ... Kd6* there follows *2 f6 Ke6 4 f×g7 Kf7 5 g×h6 b5 6 Ke4 b4 7 Kd3*) 3 f6! Resigns (if *3 ... g×f6*, then *4 h5*, and wins).

266. Pomar–Kuadras, Olot, 1974.

1 ... f4!! 2 Kd5 (*2 g×f4 is answered by 2 ... h4, and 2 e×f4 by 2 ... h4! 3 g×h4 g3! 4 f×g3 e3*) 2 ... h4! 3 K×e4 (or *3 g×h4 g3!*) 3 ... f3! 4 g×f3 h3 White resigns.

267. V. Zhuravlev–Gutman, Riga, 1974 (variation).

1 g4!! Ke5 2 g×h5 Ke6 3 h6 Kf7 4 h5 and wins. White missed this possibility, and the game ended in a draw.

268. Ditman–Padevsky, Dresden, 1956.

1 ... B×e4!! 2 f×e4 (if *2 Be2 Bd3!!*) 2 ... f3 3 g5 Ke5 4 Kc5 K×e4 5 Kb6 b4! 6 c×b4 c3 7 B×a6 c2 White resigns.

269. Shtaerman–Arkhipkin, Riga, 1974.

1 Rh8+ Kg5 2 Rg8+ Kh5 3 R×g4! K×g4 4 Kf1 (the immediate 4 b6? is bad: *4 ... f2+ 5 Kf1 Kf3*) 4 ... f4 5 g×f4 K×f4 6 b6 Resigns.

270. Sidorov–Vasiliev, Chelyabinsk, 1971.

1 ... Nb×c5!! 2 d×c5 R×b2! 3 R×b2 N×c3 4 Rc1 N×e2+ 5 Q×e2 B×b2, and Black won.

271. Tatai–Mariotti, Rome, 1972.

1 ... g4+!! 2 Q×g4 (*2 K×g4 Qf5 mate*) 2 ... Qf5!! 3 h5 c4 4 h6 Q×g4+ 5 K×g4 Kf6 White resigns.

272. Kuzmin–Hennings, Zinnovitz, 1971.

1 ... R×c6! 2 b7 Rc1+ 3 Ke2 Be4! 4 Rb2 (or *4 b8=Q Re1 mate*) 4 ... B×b7 5 R×b7 f×e5 White resigns.

Test 35   Positions 273–280

All eight positions are examples of drawing combinations. Nos. 273–276 are stalemating combinations and in Nos. 277–280 the games end in perpetual check. The time allowed is 90 minutes.

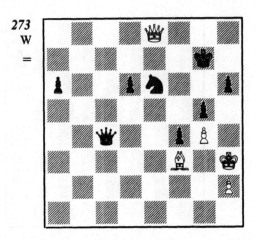

273
W
=

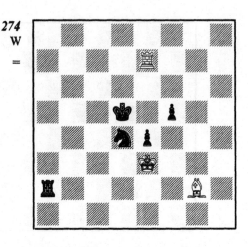

274
W
=

275
B
=

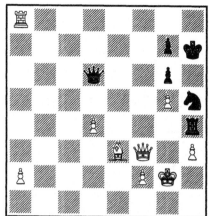

276
B
=

277
W
=

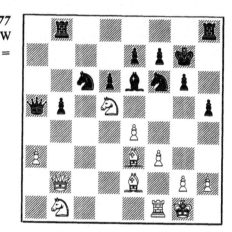

278
W
=

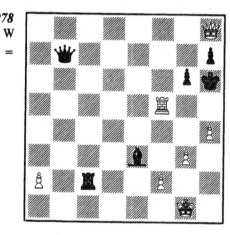

279
W
=

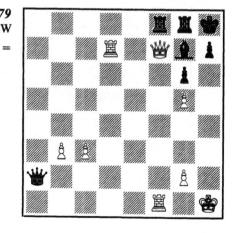

280
B
=

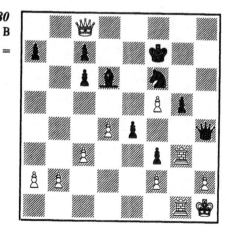

Solutions to Test 35

273. Sliwa–Doda, Warsaw, 1967.
     1 Qe7+ Kg6 (if *1 ... Kg8*, then *2 Qe8+ Nf8 3 Bd5+!! Q×d5 4 Q×f8+ K×f8* stalemate)
     2 Be4+! Q×e4 3 Qg7+ K×g7 stalemate.

274. Lisitsyn–Bondarevsky, Leningrad, 1950.
     1 B×e4+!! f×e4 2 Re5+! Kd6 (or *2 ... K×e5* stalemate) 3 R×e4—drawn.

275. Grefe–Biyiasas, Santa Monica, 1974.
     1 ... Nf4+ 2 B×f4 R×f4 3 Rd8 Rg4+! 4 Q×g4 Qg3+!!—drawn.

276. Pietzsch–Fuchs, Berlin, 1963.
     1 ... Qc6+ 2 Kf5 Ng7+! 3 B×g7 Qg6+!! 4 K×g6 stalemate.

277. Steinberg–Makarov, Kharkov, 1956.
     1 N×e7!! N×e7 (this move is forced, since everything else is worse) 2 Q×f6+!! K×f6 3
     Bd4+—drawn (*3 ... Kg5 4 Be3+* etc.).

278. Smyslov–Vasyukov, Moscow, 1961.
     1 Qf8+ Qg7 2 Rh5+!! g×h5 3 Qd6+, with a draw by perpetual check.

279. Bezenaru–S. Szabo, Gemsivar, 1956.
     1 Q×g7+!! R×g7 2 R×f8+ Rg8 3 Rff7! Rc8 4 R×h7+, and draws by perpetual check.

280. Stojanovsky–Guzel, Kragujevac, 1958.
     1 ... Q×h2+!! 2 K×h2 Ng4+ 3 Kh3 N×f2+ 4 Kh2 Ng4+, with a draw by perpetual
     check.

Test 36   Positions 281–288

A theme on which we deliberately did not touch in Book 1: 'Traps'. Each position has its own
specific problem. Fifty-five minutes are allowed for these examples, with which we expect the
reader to cope without difficulty.

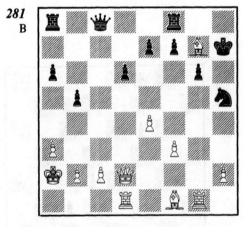

Forgetting the rule that you should not give check
without a specific aim, Black played 1 ... Qe6+? What
was the result of this?

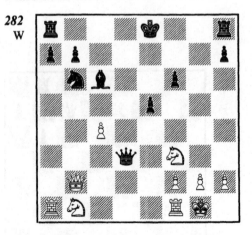

What had Black prepared against 1 Q×b6?

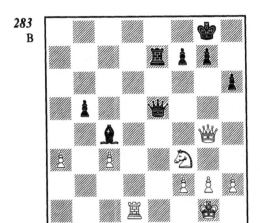

283 B

With his last move White 'courteously' invited the capture of his c3 pawn. What did he have in mind?

284 W

White is a pawn up, and his position is better. By continuing 1 B×b4 Q×b4 2 c3 Qa5 3 N×f5 he would have won easily. Instead he played 1 N×f5 immediately and fell into a trap. What was it?

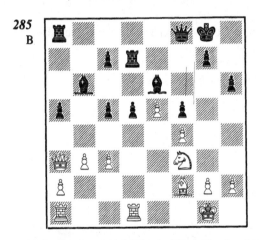

285 B

Black played 1 ... Qb8. What is this? A blunder which loses the c5 pawn, or a trap?

286 B

The position is drawn, and only one problem remains: where should White move his king after 1 ... f4+, to e4 or e2? Which is correct, and why?

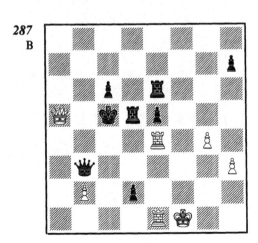

287 B

Can Black avoid the draw by playing 1 ... Qb5+?

288 B

Black unsuspectingly decided that his opponent had overlooked something, and played 1 ... Q×c2??, but thereby fell into a fairly simple trap. What was it?

Solutions to Test 36

281. Lapkin–Reshevsky, Long Beach, 1955.
    1 ... Qe6+?? 2 Bc4! Q×c4+ 3 b3! Resigns. Apart from the loss of his queen, Black is threatened with 4 Qh6+ and 5 Qh8 mate.

282. Puig–Larsson, Leipzig, 1960.
    1 Q×b6?? Q×f3!! 2 Q×c6+ (on *2 g×f3* there follows *2 ... Rg8+ 3 Kh1 B×f3* mate) 2 ... Q×c6 White resigns.

283. Ortega–Uhlmann, Polanica Zdroj, 1967.
    1 ... Q×c3?? 2 Rd8+ Kh7 3 Ng5+!! Resigns (*3 ... h×g5 4 Qh5* mate, or *3 ... Kg6 4 Ne6+ Kf6 5 Q×g7+*).

284. Peshina–Nisman, Moscow, 1968.
    1 N×f5?? Ba3!! 2 Qe7 B×b2+ 3 Kb1 Bc3+ White resigns (if *4 Kc1*, then *4 ... Rb1+!*).

285. Kostetsky–Berman, Liepaja, 1973.
    1 ... Qb8 2 B×c5?? Qf8!!, and Black won a piece and the game.

286. Pilskalnietis–Berzinsh, Aluksne, 1962.
    1 ... f4+!! 2 Ke4?? (*2 Ke2* is correct, with a draw) 2 ... Rd6!! After this move 3 R×d6 is forced, when Black has an easy win, since if 3 R×a7+, then 3 ... Ke6 and 4 ... Rd4 mate.

287. Bucher–Muller, Basel, 1959 (from a simultaneous display).
    1 ... Qb5+?? (correct is *1 ... Kd6 2 Qd8+ Kc5 3 Qa5+* etc.) 2 Rc4+!! Resigns (since if *2 ... K×c4 3 Qc3* mate or *2 ... Kd6 3 Qd8* mate).

288. Dely–Lengyel, Budapest, 1974.
    1 ... Q×c2?? 2 Nf6+!! Resigns. On 2 ... g×f6 there follows 3 Qe8+ (not *3 Rg3+? Kf8!*) 3 ... Kh7 (or *3 ... Bf8 4 Rg3+*) 4 Rg3!

Test 37 Positions 289–296

Continuation of the theme 'Traps'. This test is set for 50 minutes.

289
W

White is two pawns up, and it is hard for Black to show that he has any compensation for his material deficit. White considered that his advantage was not big enough, and he played 1 Q×d7, when he found himself in a trap. What trap?

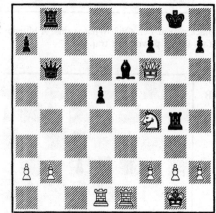

290
B

Black decided to regain his pawn by 1 ... Q×b2, but overlooked White's clever reply. What was it?

291
W

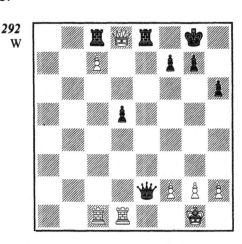

Why is 1 B×c6 bad? What had Black prepared in reply?

292
W

White thought he could win a pawn by 1 R×d5. What had he overlooked?

293
W

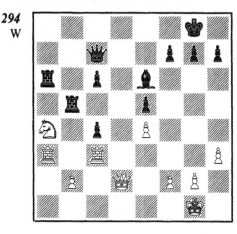

White decided to completely tie up his opponent by 1 Re×d5, but he thereby fell into a cleverly disguised trap.

294
W

White played 1 Nc5, when it seems that after 1 ... R×a3 2 R×a3 R×c5 he should lose. But is this so?

295
W

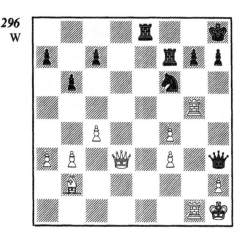

White decided to strengthen the pin, and played 1 Rf1?, but an unpleasant surprise awaited him. What was it?

296
W

Here too White decided to exploit a pin as advantageously as possible, and to this end played 1 R×g7. What trap did he fall into?

Solutions to Test 37

289. Zinn–Sveshnikov, Decin, 1974.
     1 Q×d7? Rf7!! White resigns. Any move by the queen is answered by 2 ... Bd4+.
290. Szilagyi–Szabo, Budapest, 1960.
     1 ... Q×b2?? 2 R×e6!! R×f4 (this is what Black was counting on, but ...) 3 Re8+!! Resigns.
291. Troianska–Jovanovic, Oberhausen, 1966.
     1 B×c6?? Qh1+!! White resigns.
292. Bittner–Worms, Aachen, 1954.
     1 R×d5?? R×c7!! White resigns (*2 Q×c7 Qe1+*, or *2 Rd1 R×d8*).
293. Olsen–Jakobsen, Aarus, 1953.
     1 Re×d5?? Q×g2+!! 2 K×g2 B×c6 White resigns.
294. Gancev–Pipkov, Albena, 1966.
     1 Nc5 R×a3 2 R×a3 R×c5? 3 Ra8+ Bc8 4 Ra7! Qb6 5 Qd7!! Resigns.
295. Stein–Flohr, Kiev, 1959.
     1 Rf1?? Q×f1+!! 2 B×f1 B×a2+!! White resigns.
296. Uhlmann–Dely, Budapest, 1962.
     1 R×g7?? R×g7 2 B×f6 Qg2+!! White resigns (*3 R×g2 Re1+!*).

Test 38   Positions 297–304

Fifty minutes are allowed for this test, which is again on the theme 'Traps'.

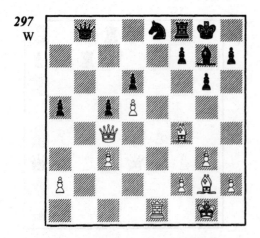

297
W

White reckoned that he could capture the c5 pawn with impunity, but is this so? What had he overlooked?

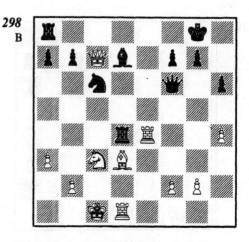

298
B

Without much thought Black made the 'obvious' move 1 ... Rc8 and, as it turned out, fell into a trap. Which?

299
B

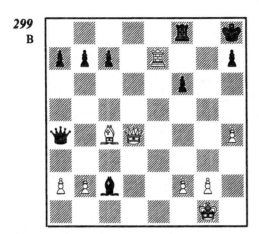

White seemed to have overlooked the possibility of 1 ... b5, but is this so?

300
W

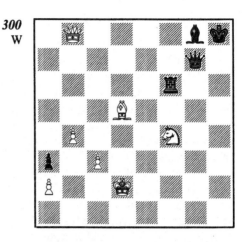

After 1 Q×g8+ Q×g8 2 B×g8 R×f4 White retains winning chances. In the game there followed 1 B×g8 Rf8. What is this, an oversight, or ...

301
W

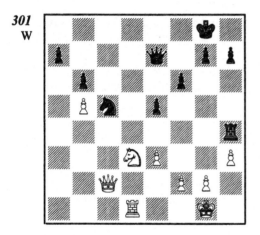

In reply to 1 Qa2+ Black made the 'natural' move 1 ... Qf7?, and fell into a trap. What was it?

302
B

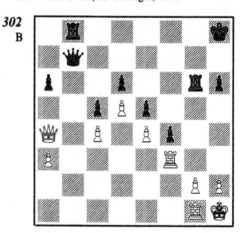

Black played 1 ... Qb2, 'courteously' inviting the opponent to invade his second rank. White unsuspectingly played 2 Qd7??, and was promptly forced to lay down his arms. What happened?

303
B

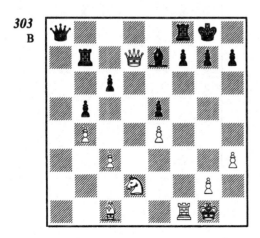

By 1 ... Qc8 Black allowed the capture of his bishop. What was the hidden point?

304
W

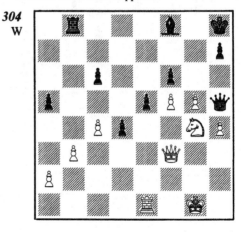

White played 1 N×e5, and Black, in turn, unsuspectingly captured with 1 ... Q×h4, but was immediately forced to resign? What happened?

Solutions to Test 38

297. Kastanga–Marcus, Bern, 1965.
     1 Q×c5?? g5! and White lost a piece. The finish was 2 R×e8 Qb1+! White resigns.

298. Olafsson–Tal, Moscow, 1971.
     1 ... Rc8?? 2 Q×c8+!! B×c8 3 Re8 mate.

299. Littlewood–Roth, Havana, 1966.
     1 ... b5?? 2 Re8!! Resigns. If 2 ... R×e8, then 3 Q×f6 mate, while on 2 ... Kg7 comes
     3 R×f8 K×f8 4 Q×f6+ Ke8 5 Bf7+ etc.

300. Izvozchikov–Ozsvath, Tbilisi, 1972.
     1 B×g8 Rf8! (after *1 ... Q×g8 2 Q×g8+ K×g8* White keeps his knight, with good win-
     ning chances) 2 Q×f8 Q×c3+!!—drawn. After 3 K×c3 it is stalemate, and likewise
     after 3 Kd1 Qd2+.

301. Bronstein–Vasyukov, Moscow, 1973.
     1 Qa2+ Qf7 2 N×e5!! Resigns.

302. Polugayevsky–Espig, Solingen, 1974.
     1 ... Qb2 2 Qd7?? Q×g2+!! White resigns (*3 R×g2 Rb1+!*).

303. Karaklajic–Boli, Sombor, 1957.
     1 ... Qc8! 2 Q×e7?? (*2 Qd3* was correct) 2 ... f6!!, and after 3 ... Rf7 White lost his queen
     and the game.

304. Karasev–Averkin, Moscow, 1967.
     1 N×e5! Q×h4? (correct was *1 ... Q×f3 2 N×f3 c5*, with equal chances) 2 Nf7+
     Resigns. On 2 ... Kg7 or 2 ... Kg8 there follows 3 Re4!, when Black loses his queen.

Test 39   Positions 305–312

We conclude the theme 'Traps'. Fifty-five minutes are allowed for this test, which is rather
more difficult than the preceding ones.

305
W

306
W

One gains the impression that after 1 N×f7 N×f7 2
Bg6 White can win a pawn. What had Black prepared
in this event?

After the plausible 1 Rd1 it appears that White should
win a piece. But is this so?

307
B

It appears that Black can play 1 ... Q×f3, but is this so?

308
B

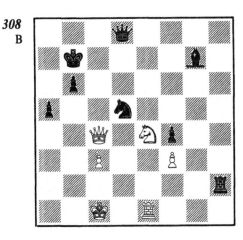

Black's position is of course easily won, but the over-hasty move 1 ... N×c3 allowed White to avoid defeat. How?

309
W

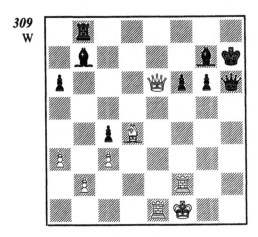

With great satisfaction White captured a pawn by 1 B×f6, but, alas, it turned out to be 'poisoned'. What was the point?

310
W

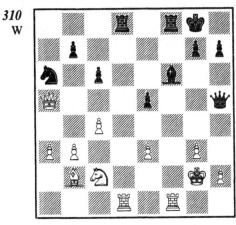

White decided to simplify by exchanging on d8, but this was a miscalculation. Why?

311
W

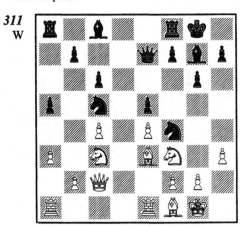

White set a trap by 1 b4. What had he prepared in the event of 1 ... a×b4?

312
W

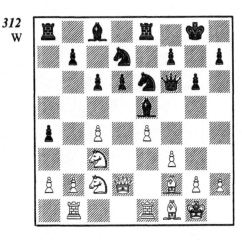

White played 1 Ne2, allowing Black to capture on b2. What was the reason for such 'generosity'?. What was concealed behind it?

Solutions to Test 39

305. Sahovic–Botvinnik, Belgrade, 1969 (variation).

1 N×f7? N×f7 2 Bg6 Ng3!! 3 B×f7 (or *3 R×d8+ N×d8*) 3 … Ne2+! and Black wins. White in fact played 1 Rh1, and the game ended in a draw.

306. Dubinsky–Bykhovsky, Moscow, 1968.

1 Rd1? Q×d1+!! 2 B×d1 R×d1+ 3 Ka2 (on *3 Kc2* there follows *3 … Rc1+!*) 3 … Nd3! White resigns.

307. Bronstein–Korchnoi, Moscow, 1962.

1 … Q×f3? 2 Rh8+ Kg6 3 R×h6+!! Resigns. Black loses his queen after 3 … g×h6 4 Qg8+ Kf6 5 Qf8+ Ke6 6 Q×f3, or 3 … K×h6 4 Qh8+ Kg6 5 Qh5+ Kf6 6 g5+!, while if 3 … Kf7 4 Qc7+ Kg8 5 Qc8+ Kf7 6 Qe6+ Kf8 7 Rh8 mate.

308. Goldin–Ryabov, Novosibirsk, 1972.

1 … N×c3?? 2 Nd6+! Q×d6 (*2 … Ka7 3 Re7+!*) 3 Re7+! Q×e7 4 Qc7+! K×c7— stalemate.

309. Panek–Grushka, Marianska-Lazne, 1956.

1 B×f6?? Re8!! 2 Q×e8 Qh3+ 3 Ke2 Qd3 mate.

310. Mititelu–Stancu, Bucharest, 1963.

1 R×d8?? Qe2+!! (an unexpected zwischenzug) 2 Rf2 Q×f2+!! 3 K×f2 B×d8+! White resigns. On 2 Kg1 there follows 2 … Q×f1+, with the same idea.

311. Letelier–Bolbochan, Mar del Plata, 1959.

1 b4! a×b4?? 2 B×c5! Q×c5 3 a×b4 Resigns.

312. Reshevsky–Najdorf, Helsinki, 1952.

1 Ne2! B×b2? 2 R×b2! Q×b2 3 Nc3! and White won the black queen. The finish was 3 … a3 4 Rb1 Ndc5 5 R×b2 a×b2 6 Nb4 Na4 7 Nb1 Bd7 8 Nd3 b5 9 c×b5 c×b5 10 N×b2, and Black resigned.

Test 40   Positions 313–320

Theme: 'Combinations based on geometrical motifs' (cf. schematic diagrams Nos. 385, 386 and 378 in Book 1). A relatively simple test, for which you are allowed 60 minutes.

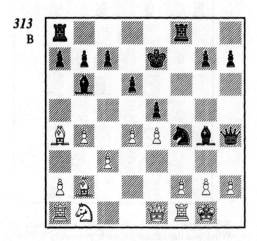

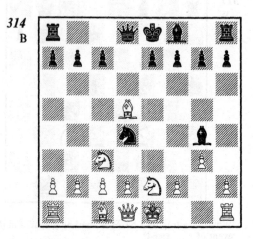

315
B

316
W

317
W

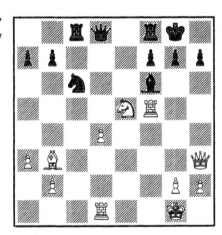

318
W

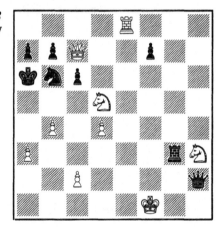

319
W

320
B

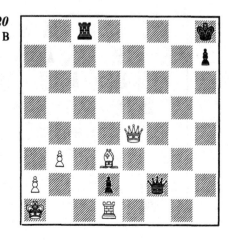

Solutions to Test 40

313. Larsson–Enevoldsen, Corr., 1968.
    1 ... Qh3!! 2 g×h3 Bf3! White resigns. There is no defence against 3 ... N×h3 mate.
314. Gibbs–Schmid, Lugano, 1968.
    1 ... Q×d5!! 2 N×d5 Nf3+ 3 Kf1 Bh3 mate.
315. Teplov–Baldin, Moscow, 1959.
    1 ... Nh3+!! 2 Kh1 Q×f3! 3 g×f3 B×f3 mate.
316. Spassky–Korchnoi, Kiev, 1968.
    1 Qh6+!! Resigns (*1 ... K×h6 2 Rh1* mate, or *1 ... Kg8 2 Rc8+*).
317. Kogan–Foster, Boston, 1947.
    1 Q×h7+!! K×h7 2 Rh5+ Kg8 3 Ng6 Resigns.
318. Mustonen–Sorakunas, Helsinki, 1968.
    1 Q×b6+!! a×b6 2 Nc7+ Ka7 3 Ra8 mate.
319. Matulovic–Sakharov, Sukhumi, 1966.
    1 Ne6!! Rae8 (if 1 ... *f×e6*, then *2 f×e6+ f5 3 Qf4 Qb1+ 4 Nc1 Rf8 5 R×g8!* and wins)
    2 R×g8! R×g8 3 Q×h6+!! K×h6 4 Rh3 mate.
320. Fernandez–Lommer, Venice, 1967.
    1 ... Qf6+ 2 Kb1 Rc1+ 3 R×c1 Qa1+!! 4 K×a1 d×c1=Q+ 5 Bb1 Qc3 mate.

Test 41   Positions 321–328

Continuation of the theme 'Mating combinations based on geometrical motifs' (cf. schematic diagrams Nos. 377, 380 and 383 in Book 1). The solving time allowed is 60 minutes.

321
W

322
W

323
W

324
B

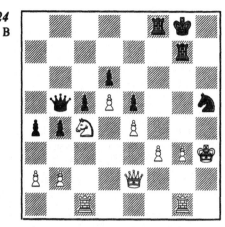

325
W

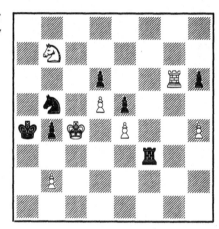

326
B

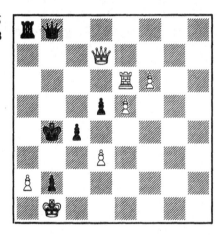

327
W

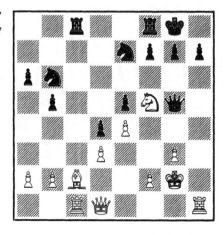

328
B

Solutions to Test 41

321. Ageichenko–Shilov, Moscow, 1970.
    1 Nf6+!! g×f6 2 Qg4+ Kh7 3 Ree3!! Resigns. There is no defence against 4 R×h6+ and 5 Rh3 mate.

322. Suetin–N.N., Moscow, 1965 (from a simultaneous display).
    1 Qg4! g6 2 Qe6+!! Kh8 3 Qf6+!! Resigns.

323. Budrich–Gumprich, Berlin, 1950.
    1 B×d5+! c×d5 2 Q×f8+!! K×f8 3 Rc8+ Bd8 4 R×d8 mate.

324. Vestin–Karlsson, Stockholm, 1973.
    1 ... Kf7!! 2 N×d6+ Ke7 3 N×b5 Nf4+! 4 g×f4 Rh8 mate.

325. Nedeljkovic–Udovcic, Zagreb, 1952 (variation).
    1 b3+!! R×b3 2 Nc5+!! d×c5 3 Ra6 mate. White overlooked this possibility, and the game concluded 1 Rg8?? Na3+!! 2 b×a3 Rc3 mate.

326. Dumitru–Kusmin, Konstanza, 1972.
    1 ... Kc3!! 2 Q×d5 Qb3!! 3 Q×c4+ Q×c4 4 d×c4 Rh8! White resigns.

327. Durao–Ben Rakhuma, Lugano, 1968.
    1 Qh5!! Q×h5 2 N×e7+ Kh8 3 R×h5 Rc7 (intending after the knight moves to play ... Rfc8, but ...) 4 R×h7+!! K×h7 5 Rh1 mate.

328. Meo–Giustolisi, Reggio Emilia, 1959.
    1 ... Ne2+ 2 Kh1 Q×h2+!! 3 K×h2 Rh4 mate.

Test 42   Positions 329–336

Some further examples on the theme 'Mating combinations based on geometrical motifs' (cf. Nos. 379 and 384 in Book 1). This test is timed for 55 minutes.

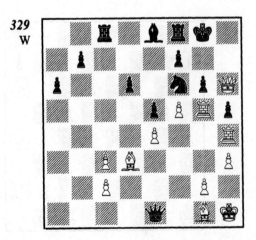

329
W

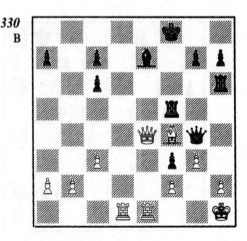

330
B

331
W

332
W

333
B

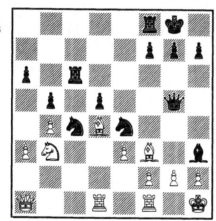

334
W

335
W

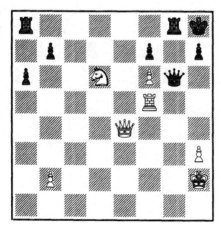

336
W

Solutions to Test 42

329. Bouzaiz–Weiss, Lugano, 1968.
  1 R h×h5!! N×h5 2 R×h5! g×h5 3 Qg5+ Kh7 4 f6 Resigns.
330. Grabow–Kunde, East Germany.
  1 ... R×h2+!! 2 K×h2 Rh5+ 3 Kg1 Rh1+! 4 K×h1 Qh3+ 5 Kg1 Qg2 mate.
331. Panno–Malich, Munich, 1958.
  1 B×e5 R×c2 (*1 ... B×e5 or 1 ... d×e5 is met by 2 Nc6!, when the threat of 3 Ne7+ wins the exchange*) 2 B×g7!! R×c1 3 Bf6!! Kf8 4 Q×c1 Ke8 5 Qc7 Resigns (on *5 ... Qb7 there follows 6 Q×d6*).
332. Rein–Klish, Corr., 1962.
  1 R×g7+!! K×g7 2 Rg1+ Kh8 3 Q×e8+!! R×e8 4 N×f7 mate.
333. Balanel–Pytljakowski, Marianske Lazne, 1951.
  1 ... Rg6!! 2 g×h3 (if *2 g3 B×f1 3 R×f1 Ncd2!*) 2 ... Qg1+!! 3 R×g1 N×f2 mate.
334. Kurajica–Ujtelky, Beverwijk, 1969.
  1 Ng6+!! Kg8 (or *1 ... f×g6 2 f×g6!*) 2 Qe8+! Kh7 3 Qh8+!! B×h8 4 Nf8 mate.
335. Suta–Suteu, Bucharest, 1953.
  1 Rg5!! Q×f6 (*1 ... Q×e4 2 N×f7 mate*) 2 Qd4!! Rg6 3 R×g6! Resigns.
336. Alekseyev–Veksler, Liepaja, 1972.
  1 Nf6!! g6 2 N×e8!! g×f5 3 Rd8! Qe7 4 Nd6+! Q×d8 5 N×f7 mate. In the game White played 4 Rc8??, and after 4 ... Q×e8 he lost.

Test 43   Positions 337–344

Conclusion of the theme 'Mating combinations based on gemoetrical motifs' (cf. schematic diagram No. 382 in Book 1). Seventy minutes are allowed for this test, which is quite difficult.

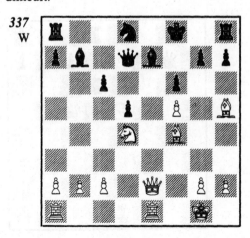

337
W

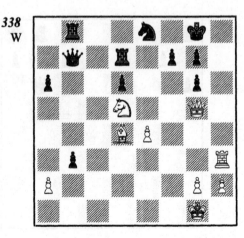

338
W

339
W

340
W

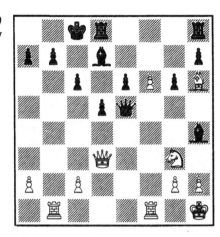

341
W

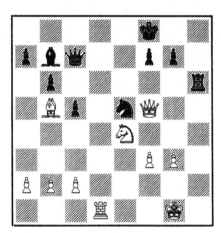

342
W

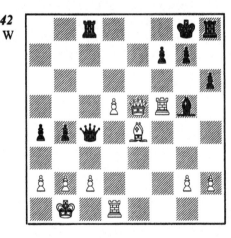

343
W

344
B

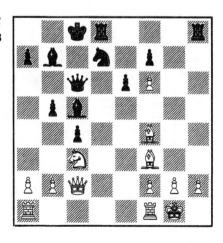

Solutions to Test 43

337. Gligoric–Rosenstein, USA, 1963.
     1 Q×e7+!! Q×e7 2 Bd6! Q×d6 3 Re8 mate.
338. Sämisch–N.N., Bern, 1949 (from a blindfold simultaneous display).
     1 Nf6+!! N×f6 (*1 ... g×f6 2 Qh6!*, or *1 ... Kf8 2 Rh8+ Ke7 3 Nd5++ Ke6 4 Nf4* mate)
     2 Q×f6!! g×f6 3 B×f6 Resigns.
339. Byelov–Osadchuk, Omsk, 1965.
     1 Qf8+!! K×f8 (or *1 ... Kg6 2 Qh6* mate) 2 Bh6+ Kg8 3 Re8 mate.
340. Estrin–Rudensky, Moscow, 1947.
     1 Bf4!! Q×f6 2 Qa6! b×a6 3 Rb8 mate.
341. King–Bedian, California, 1962.
     1 Q×e5!! Q×e5 2 Rd8+ Ke7 3 Re8 mate.
342. Ivkov–Inrerslev, Moscow, 1956.
     1 R×f7!! K×f7 2 Qe6+ Kf8 3 Bg6 Qc7 4 Re1 Resigns (against *5 Qe8+! R×e8 6 R×e8*
     mate there is no defence).
343. Hepner–Gode, London, 1963.
     1 N×g5+!! h×g5 (declining the sacrifice is no better: *1 ... Kg6 2 Be4+ K×g5 3 R×g7+*,
     or *2 ... Kh5 3 R×g7*, and wins) 2 Be4+ Kh6 3 Rh8+! B×h8 4 Rh7 mate.
344. Johansson–Ekenberg, Sweden, 1974.
     1 ... Q×f3!! 2 g×f3 Rdg8+ 3 Bg3 R×g3+!! 4 h×g3 B×f3 White resigns.

Test 44   Positions 345–352

A new theme: 'Attack on the K-side castled position'. This test is set for 45 minutes.

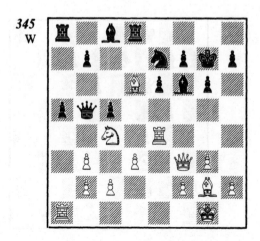

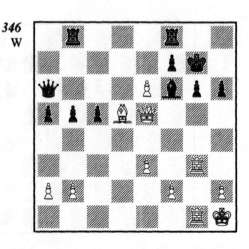

347
B

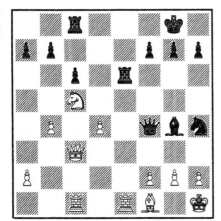

348
W

349
B

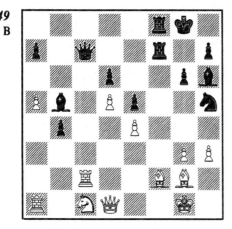

350
W

351
B

352
B

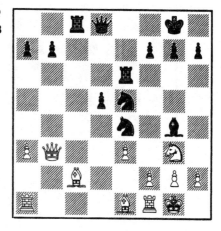

Solutions to Test 44

345. Petrosian–Pachman, Bled, 1961.
    1 Q×f6+!! K×f6 2 Be5+ Kg5 3 Bg7! Resigns (there is no defence against mate by *4 h4+* and *5 Bf3* or *5 Bh3*).
346. Quinteros–Henley, Lone Pine, 1976.
    1 R×g6+! f×g6 2 R×g6+! K×g6 3 Be4+! Kg7 4 Qc7+ Resigns.
347. Furman–Klovan, Kaliningrad, 1964.
    1 ... Nf3!! 2 g3 (or *2 g×f3 Rh6! 3 h3 B×f3+ 4 Bg2 R×h3+*) 2 ... Rh6! 3 h3 R×h3+! 4 B×h3 Qh6! White resigns.
348. Winter–Winiwater, Vienna, 1967.
    1 Rf7! b×c4 (after *1 ... K×f7 2 Ne7+ Kf8 3 N×c8 R×c8 4 Q×h7* the advance of the h-pawn is decisive) 2 Bf6!! K×f7 (forced) 3 Nh8++!! Resigns (since *3 ... K×f6 4 Qh4* is mate).
349. Stor–Yudovich, Corr., 1959.
    1 ... R×f2!! 2 R×c7 Be3!! White resigns. The alternatives were 3 Kh2 R×g2+ 4 K×g2 Rf2+, 3 Qb3 Bf1! 4 Q×e3 R×g2+ 5 Kh1 N×g3+ 6 Q×g3 R×g3 and wins, or 3 Nd3 Rf1++ 4 Kh2 Bg1+ 5 Kh1 N×g3 mate.
350. Spassky–Schmidt, Varna, 1962.
    1 Bd3! Q×c5 (or *1 ... B×d3 2 Qh7+ Kf8 3 Nce6+!! f×e6 4 d×e6*) 2 B×f5 N×d5 (if *2 ... g×f5 3 Qh7+ Kf8 4 Qh5!*) 3 Be6!! Resigns.
351. Averbakh–Kholmov, Riga, 1970.
    1 ... Bh3! 2 g3 Rd3! 3 Qc2 Qe4 4 f3 R×d1+! White resigns (*5 Q×d1 Q×e3+ 6 Kh1 Qf2* and wins).
352. Ojanen–Kinmark, Turku, 1967.
    1 ... Nf3+! 2 g×f3 Qh4!! 3 f×g4 Rh6 4 Kg2 (on *4 Nh5* there follows *4 ... Q×g4+ 5 Ng3 Qh4!*) 4 ... Ng5! White resigns (*5 Rh1 Qh3+ 6 Kh1 Nf3* mate).

Test 45   Positions 353–360

Continuation and conclusion of the preceding theme. The time for completing this test is 45 minutes.

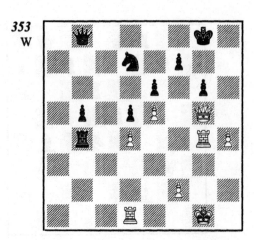

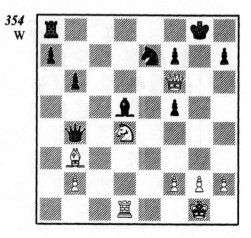

355
B

356
W

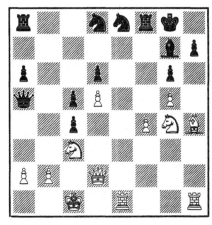

357
W

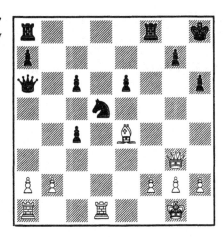

358
W

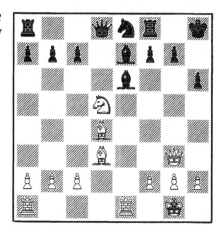

359
B

360
W

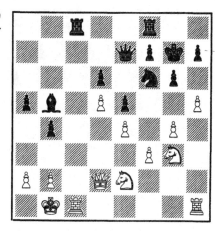

Solutions to Test 45

353. Kircek–Tomic, Dortmund, 1978.

     1 h5! Nf8 (*1 … Qe8 2 h×g6 f×g6 3 Qh6! and wins*) 2 Qe7! Rc4 3 h6 Nh7 (*3 … Rc7 4 Qf6*) 4 R×g6+! Kh8 5 Q×f7 Resigns.

354. Tal–Tolush, Riga, 1958.

     1 Nc6!! Q×b3 (*1 … B×c6 is met by 2 Q×f7+ Kh8 3 Qf6 mate, and 1 … N×c6 by 2 B×d5*) 2 N×e7+ Kf8 3 Re1!! Be6 4 N×f5 Resigns.

355. Keres–Petrosian, Bled, 1959.

     1 … Rg3!! 2 h×g3 h×g3 3 Rfd2 Qh4 4 Be2 Rh7 5 Kf1 (*5 Bh5 is no better: 5 … R×h5 6 Kf1 Nd3 7 R×d3 e×d3 8 Q×d3 Qh1+ and 9 … Q×g2+*) 5 … Q×f4+!! White resigns.

356. Szabo–Orban, Szczawno Zdroj, 1957.

     1 Nf6+!! N×f6 2 g×f6 B×f6 3 B×f6 R×f6 4 Re8+ Kg7 (or *4 … Kf7 5 Qe3!!*) 5 R×h7+! Resigns (there is no defence against *Qh2+*, *Qh8+* and *Qf8 mate*).

357. Witkowski–Gromek, Poland, 1967.

     1 Qg6! Nf6 2 Rd7! Rg8 3 Q×f6!! Rae8 4 Q×h6+! Resigns.

358. Udovcic–Bertok, Zagreb, 1954.

     1 R×e6! Q×d5 (or *1 … f×e6 2 Qg6!*) 2 R×h6+! Kg8 3 Rh8+! K×h8 4 Qh3+ Kg8 5 Qh7 mate.

359. Barcza–Matanovic, Moscow, 1956.

     1 … R×d4!! 2 R×c8+ N×c8 3 Qc2 R×g4+!! 4 h×g4 Nf3+ 5 Kg2 Q×g4+ White resigns.

360. Keller–Schtechlik, Vienna, 1952.

     1 Nf5+! g×f5 2 Qg5+ Kh8 3 h6 R×c1+ 4 R×c1 Rg8 5 Rc8!! Resigns (*5 … Be8 is answered by 6 R×e8!*).

Test 46   Positions 361–368

Theme: 'Attack on the king caught in the centre'. To this theme we devote four tests, since players frequently fail to utilize such opportunities. This test is timed for 75 minutes.

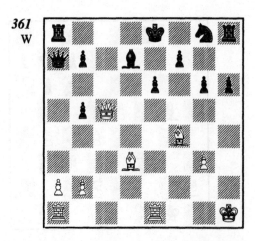

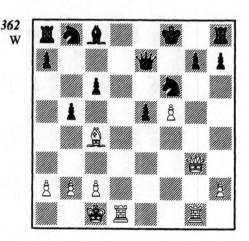

363
W
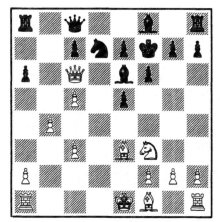

364
W
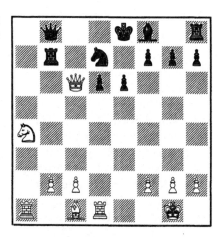

365
B

366
B

367
B
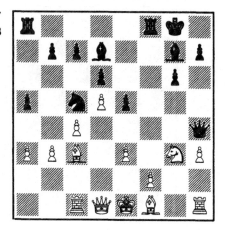

368
W
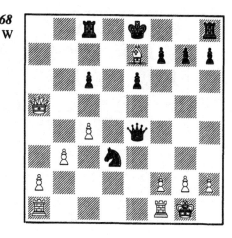

Solutions to Test 46

361. Rodriguez–Miyaska, Skopje, 1972.
    1 R×e6+!! f×e6 (or *1 ... B×e6 2 B×b5+ Bd7 3 Re1+!*) 2 B×g6+ Kd8 3 Qf8+ Resigns.

362. Vishnyatsky–Perevoznikov, Tashkent, 1950.
    1 Rd8+! Ne8 2 f6! Q×f6 (*2 ... g×f6 3 Qg8+!*) 3 Qa3+ Resigns (on *3 ... Qe7* there follows *4 R×g7! Q×a3 5 Rf7+ Kg8 6 R×e8+*).

363. Matsukevich–Bodisko, Tula, 1959.
    1 Q×e6+!! K×e6 2 Bc4+ Kf5 3 Nh4+ Ke4 (if *3 ... Kg4*, then *4 g3* followed by *5 h3* mate) 4 Ke2 Resigns (there is no defence against *5 f3* mate).

364. Smyslov–Kottnauer, Groningen, 1946.
    1 Nc5!! d×c5 2 Bf4 Bd6 (or *2 ... Q×f4 3 Qc8+ Ke7 4 Q×b7*) 3 B×d6 Rb6 4 Q×d7+! Resigns (*4 ... K×d7 5 B×b8+*).

365. Mogordoev–Kuznetsov, Gorky, 1963.
    1 ... R×d3+!! 2 K×d3 Bf5+ 3 Kc3 Na4+ 4 Kb3 Nd4+ 5 K×a4 Bc2+ White resigns (*6 Ka5 Nc6+ 7 Kb5 a6+ 8 Kc5 Be4* followed by *9 ... b6* mate).

366. Franklin–Wade, Hastings, 1961.
    1 ... B×c3!! 2 B×c3 R×e3+! 3 K×e3 (or *3 Kd2 Rf2+!*) 3 ... Qg3+ 4 Kd4 (*4 Kd2 Rf2+ 5 Ke1 Qe3+*) 4 ... Q×g4+ 5 K×d5 Rd8+ White resigns.

367. Larsen–Portisch, Siegen, 1970.
    1 ... R×f2!! 2 K×f2 Ne4+ 3 Kg1 Q×g3+ 4 Bg2 Q×e3+ White resigns. After 5 Kh2 Qg3+ 6 Kg1 Bh6 he cannot avoid further losses.

368. Taimanov–Steiner, Stockholm, 1952.
    1 Rad1! Qf5 (other continuations similarly fail to save the game, e.g. *1 ... K×e7 2 Qg5+ Kf8 3 Rfe1 Qd4 4 Qd2 Rd8 5 Re3*, or here *2 ... Ke8 3 Qd2 Nc5 4 Qd6!*, or *1 ... f5 2 Qa7 c5 3 Bg5!*) 2 Qa7 Resigns.

Test 47   Positions 369–376

Seventy minutes are allowed for this test, which is of similar difficulty to the previous one.

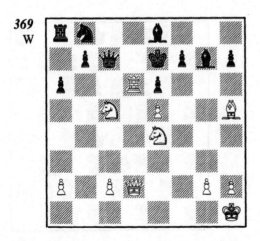

369
W

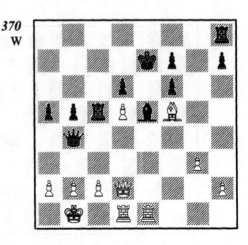

370
W

371
W

372
B

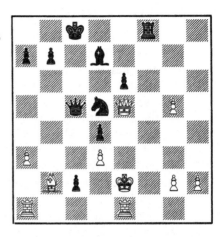

373
W

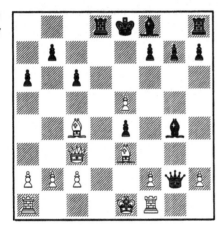

374
W

375
W

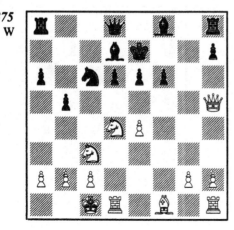

376
W

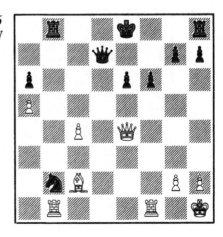

Solutions to Test 47

369. Timman–Quinteros, Amsterdam, 1973.
   1 R×e6+!! Kf8 (*1 ... f×e6* fails to *2 Qg5+ Kf8 3 N×e6+*) 2 R×e8+!! K×e8 3 Ne6! Qc6 4 Nd6+ Resigns (*4 ... Ke7 5 Nc8+*, or *4 ... Kd7 5 Nc4+*).

370. Tal–Malich, East Germany, 1957.
   1 R×e5+!! f×e5 (or *1 ... d×e5 2 d6+*) 2 Qg5+ Kf8 (on *2 ... Ke8* White would have continued as in the game) 3 Qf6! Rg8 4 Be6! Resigns.

371. Bastrikov–Kagan, Minsk, 1971.
   1 e5! d×e5 2 Nc×b5! Qb6 (or *2 ... a×b5 3 B×b5+ Ke7 4 Nf5+!! e×f5 5 R×e5+*) 3 N×e6! f×e6 4 Bg6+ Resigns.

372. Lutzkat–Netzold, East Germany, 1972.
   1 ... Nc3+ 2 Kd2 Nb1+ 3 Kc1 (if *3 Ra×b1 c×b1=N+!*) 3 ... Q×e5 4 R×e5 Rf1+ White resigns (*5 K×c2 Ba4* mate).

373. Wilhelm–Fetscher, East Germany, 1973.
   1 ... Qf3! 2 Bd2 Bb4!! 3 Q×b4 (or *3 B×f7+ Q×f7!*) 3 ... Rd3! 4 B×f7+ K×f7 5 Q×b7+ Kg6 White resigns.

374. Mikenas–Lebedev, Tbilisi, 1947.
   1 Ng4+!! h×g4 (*1 ... Kg7 2 Qh7* mate, or *1 ... Ke7 2 Qd6* mate) 2 Be5+! K×e5 3 Qd4 mate.

375. Drapper–Leonhardt, Corr., 1964/65.
   1 Nf5+!! e×f5 2 Nd5+ Ke6 3 e×f5+ Ke5 4 Bc4 Resigns.

376. Duckstein–Pachman, Varna, 1962.
   1 Ba4! Q×a4 2 Q×e6+ Kd8 (on *2 ... Kf8* there follows *3 R×f6+ g×f6 4 Q×f6+ Kg8 5 Qg5+ Kf7 6 Rf1+*) 3 Qd6+ Kc8 4 Rf5 Resigns.

Test 48   Positions 377–384

Continuation of the theme 'Attack on the king caught in the centre'. Rather more difficult than the two preceding tests. Solving time 70 minutes.

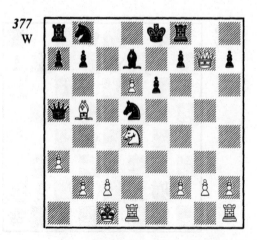

377
W

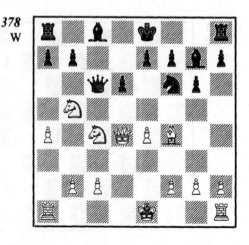

378
W

379
B

380
W

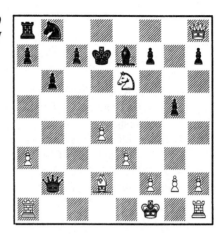

381
W

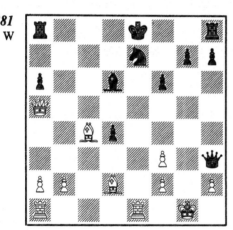

382
W

383
W

384
B

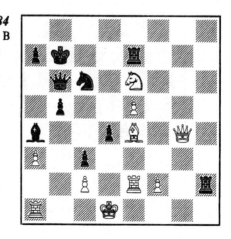

Solutions to Test 48

377. Belyaev–Silaev, Corr., 1976.
1 N×e6! f×e6 2 R×d5! Qd8 3 Rf5! Resigns (*3 ... e×f5 4 Re1+ or 3 ... R×f5 4 Qg8+ Rf8 5 Q×e6+*).

378. Eisinger Kristof, Waldkirch, 1968.
1 Nc×d6+! e×d6 (*1 ... Kf8 2 N×c8*) 2 N×d6+ Ke7 (*2 ... Kf8 is bad in view of 3 Bh6!*) 3 Qb4! Resigns.

379. Zubkov–Zarenin, Sevastopol, 1968.
1 ... R×d3!! 2 Q×d3 Bf2+ 3 Ke2 (or *3 Kf1 Rd8 4 Qe2 Rd1+! 5 Q×d1 N×e4*) 3 ... Rd8 4 Qc2 Nh5! White resigns.

380. Milev–Bobekov, Sofia, 1957.
1 Ng7! Q×a1+ 2 Ke2 Q×a3 (the result is not affected by *2 ... Q×h1 3 Qe8+ Kd6 4 Nf5+ Ke6 5 Q×e7+ K×f5 6 Q×f7+ Kg4 7 Qf3+ Kh4 8 Qh3 mate*, while *2 ... Nc6 is equally bad in view of 3 Q×a8 Q×h1 4 Qe8+ Kd6 5 Bb4+! N×b4 6 Nf5+*) 3 Qe8+ Kd6 4 Ra1!! Q×a1 5 Nf5+ Resigns.

381. Tseitlin–Krutyansky, Leningrad, 1971.
1 R×e7+! K×e7 (or *1 ... B×e7 2 Qd5 Rd8 3 Qf7+ Kd7 4 Re1 and wins*) 2 Re1+ Kf8 3 Bf4 g6 4 Qd5! Resigns.

382. Pati–Frenkel, USA, 1973.
1 N×h6! g×h6 2 R×f7+ Kd6 3 Qh5! Bd7 4 Q×e5+! K×e5 5 Bf4 mate.

383. Botvinnik–Euwe, The Hague/Moscow, 1948.
1 Qg3! f×e5 2 Qg7 Rf8 3 Rc7! Q×c7 4 Q×c7, and White won.

384. Dahl–Walbom, Stockholm, 1968.
1 ... d3! 2 B×c6+! (or *2 B×d3 Rh1+ 3 Re1 Q×f2!!*) 2 ... Q×c6! 3 Nd8+ Kc7 4 N×c6 Rh1+ 5 Re1 B×c2+ White resigns.

Test 49   Positions 385–392

The final test on this theme. The time allotted is 70 minutes.

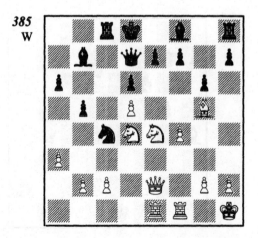

385
W

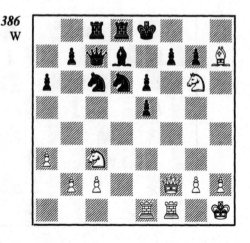

386
W

387
W

388
W

389
W

390
W

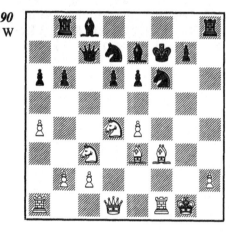

391
W

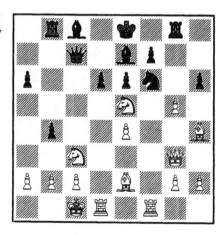

392
B

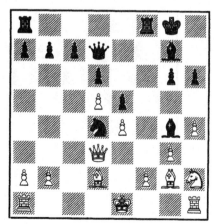

Solutions to Test 49

385. Alfoldi–Sagi, Debrecen, 1955.
   1 Nf6!! Qc7 2 Qe6!! Ne5 3 Q×f7!! Qd7 4 f×e5 Resigns.
386. Rusakov–Kalinkin, Omsk, 1963.
   1 Q×f7+!! N×f7 2 R×f7! K×f7 3 Rf1+ Ke8 4 Rf8 mate.
387. Geller–Nilsson, Stockholm, 1954.
   1 Rd8+! R×d8 2 Re1+ Kf8 3 Q×d8+ Kg7 4 Re7! Resigns.
388. Radayev–Akhmedov, Baku, 1973.
   1 Bb6!! a×b6 2 R×e6+! Ne7 3 Q×f7+ Kd8 4 Qe8+!! K×e8 5 B×g6 mate.
389. Doda–Lanzias, Varna, 1962.
   1 Bd7!! R×d7 2 R×d7 Qc6 (there is no satisfactory defence) 3 Re7+! K×e7 4 Q×c6 b×c6 5 Nd4 Resigns.
390. Pflughaupt–Galander, Munster, 1954.
   1 N×e6!! K×e6 2 Qd5+!! N×d5 3 Bg4+ Ke5 4 Rf5+ Ke6 5 e×d5 mate.
391. Grefe–Browne, USA, 1973.
   1 N×f7!! b×c3 (or *1 ... K×f7 2 Bh5+ Kf8 3 g×f6! R×g3 4 f×e7+*) 2 g×f6!! R×g3 3 f×e7 Rg5 4 B×g5 h×g5 5 N×d6+ Resigns.
392. Dashinimayev–Motilev, Sverdlovsk, 1974.
   1 ... R×f2!! 2 K×f2 Rf8+ 3 Ke1 (or *3 Kg1 Ne2+!*) 3 ... Qb5!! 4 Bf1 (or *4 Q×b5 Nc2 mate*) 4 ... N×c2+!! 5 Q×c2 R×f1+!! White resigns.

Test 50   Positions 393–400

Theme: 'Destructive combinations', i.e. combinations whose aim is to destroy the opposing king's pawn cover. The solving time for this test is 70 minutes.

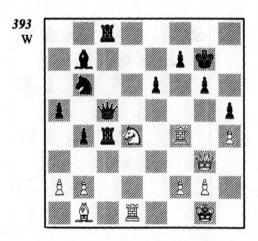

393
W

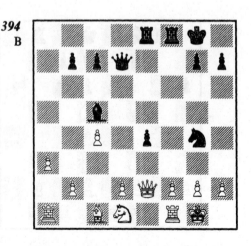

394
B

395
B

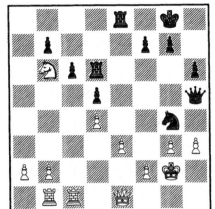

396
W

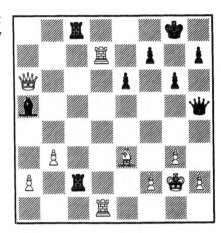

397
B

398
W

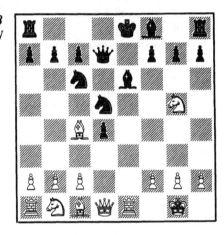

399
B

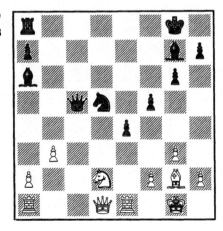

400
W

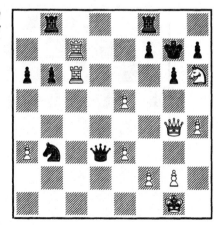

Solutions to Test 50

393. Mishuchkov–Khavsky, Leningrad, 1968.
    1 R×f7+!! K×f7 2 Q×g6+ Ke7 3 Nc6+! Resigns. Whatever Black captures with on c6, there follows 4 Qg7+ and 5 Bg6 mate.
394. Kuster–Kislov, Corr., 1970.
    1 ... R×f2!! 2 N×f2 Rf8 3 Q×e4 N×f2 4 Qe2 Qg4!! White resigns.
395. Fuster–Simagin, Moscow, 1949.
    1 ... N×f2!! 2 Q×f2 (if *2 K×f2*, then *2 ... Rf6+ 3 Kg1 Rf3*) 2 ... Rf6 3 Qg1 (or *3 Qd2 Qf3+*) 3 ... Qe2+ 4 Kh1 Rf2! White resigns.
396. Weiss–Herzog, Corr., 1963.
    1 R×f7!! Q×d1 (if *1 ... K×f7 2 Rd7+ Kf6 3 Bd4+ Kf5 4 Qd3+*) 2 Q×e6 Qa1 (on *2 ... R2c6* there follows *3 Rf8++ K×f8 4 Bh6* mate) 3 Rc7+ Kh8 4 Q×c8 mate.
397. Zita–Taimanov, Szczawno Zdroj, 1950.
    1 ... N×f2! 2 K×f2 Qh3! 3 Rd4 Q×h2+ 4 Bg2 R×e3 5 N×d5 Q×g3+ White resigns (*6 Kg1 Re1+ 7 R×e1 Q×e1+ 8 Kh2 c×d5*).
398. Senelt–Mayer, Berlin, 1958.
    1 N×f7!! Bb4 (if *1 ... Q×f7 2 B×d5*, while on *1 ... K×f7* there follows *2 Qf3+ Kg6—* or *2 ... Kg8 3 R×e6 Q×e6 4 B×d5—3 R×e6! Q×e6 4 Bd3+*) 2 c3 0-0 3 Ng5 d×c3 4 R×e6 Resigns.
399. Delmar–Messing, Monte Carlo, 1957.
    1 ... Q×f2+!! 2 K×f2 (or *2 Kh1 B×a1*) 2 ... Bd4+ 3 Re3 N×e3 4 Nc4 (or *4 Ke1 N×g2* mate) 4 ... N×d1+ White resigns.
400. Geller–Kholmov, Bad Salzbrunn, 1957.
    1 N×f7!! R×f7 2 R×f7+ K×f7 3 Rc7+ Kf8 4 Qe6! Resigns.

Test 51   Positions 401–408

Continuation of the theme 'Destructive combinations'. The solving time for this test is 60 minutes.

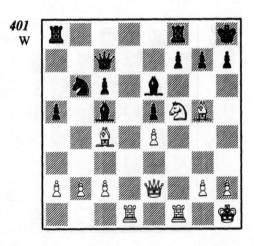

401
W

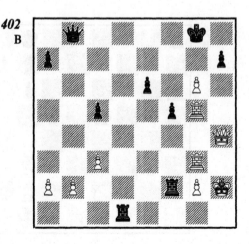

402
B

403
W

404
B
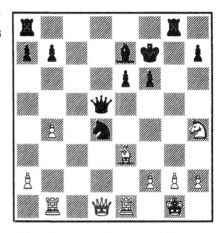

405
B

406
W

407
B
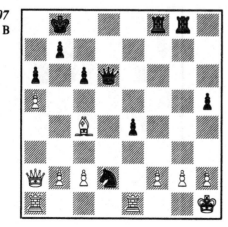

408
W
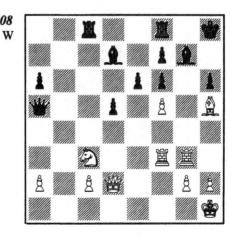

Solutions to Test 51

401. Stein–Portisch, Stockholm, 1962.
    1 N×g7!! B×c4 (or *1 ... K×g7 2 Bf6+ Kg8 3 Qd2 Rfd8 4 Qh6 Bf8 5 Qg5+*) 2 Bf6!! Be7 (if *2 ... B×e2*, then *3 Nf5+ Kg8 4 Nh6* mate) 3 Qf3 Resigns.

402. Schotenheim–Hazeman, Corr., 1958.
    1 ... R×g2+!! 2 K×g2 Q×b2+ 3 Kf3 Q×c3+ White resigns.

403. Lipnitsky–Kolterman, Kharkov, 1950.
    1 R×g7!! c×d4 (or *1 ... K×g7 2 Rg1+ K×h7 3 Qg2*) 2 Rhg1! Bf8 (if *2 ... Bb7*, then *3 Rg8+ R×g8 4 h×g8=Q+ R×g8 5 Qh6* mate) 3 Qh6 Resigns.

404. Zilic–Pfankuche, Buenos Aires, 1957.
    1 ... R×g2+!! 2 Kf1 (*2 N×g2 is answered by 2 ... Rg8 3 f3 N×f3+ 4 Kh1 R×g2! 5 K×g2 Nh4++ 6 Kg3 Qg2+! 7 K×h4 f5+ 8 Kh5 Qg6* mate) 2 ... Rg1+! 3 K×g1 Rg8+ White resigns.

405. Vorobyev–Klampus, Corr., 1960.
    1 ... B×g2+!! 2 K×g2 Rf2+ 3 Kh1 R×h2+!! 4 K×h2 Rf2+ 5 Kh1 Q×g3 White resigns.

406. Furman–Konstantinopolsky, Moscow, 1948.
    1 R×g7+!! K×g7 2 Qc3+ Kh6 (or *2 ... Kg8 3 Nf6+*) 3 R×f7 Q×d5 4 Qf6+ Kh5 5 R×h7+ Resigns.

407. Parma–Damjanovic, Zagreb, 1960.
    1 ... R×g2!! 2 K×g2 Qg6+ 3 Kh1 R×f2 4 Rg1 Nf3! White resigns.

408. Parma–Ramirez, Malaga, 1963.
    1 R×g7! K×g7 2 Rg3+ Kh7 3 Bg6+ Kg7 4 Bh7+! Resigns (*4 ... K×h7 5 Rh3!*).

Test 52   Positions 409–416

This test, a continuation of the preceding theme, includes various forms of these combinations. It is similar in difficulty to the previous test, and so the time allotted is again 60 minutes.

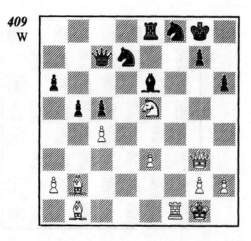

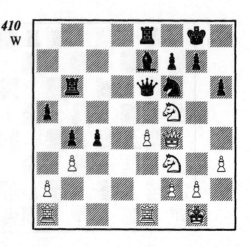

411
W

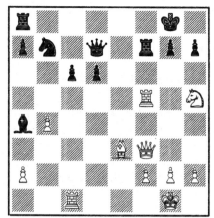

412
W

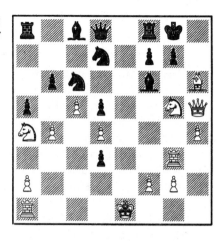

413
W

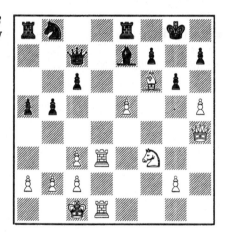

414
W

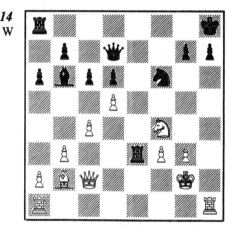

415
W

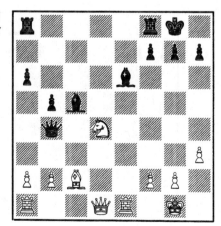

416
W

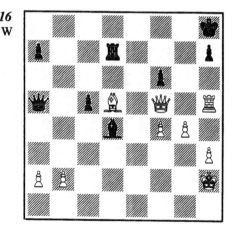

TYC—H

Solutions to Test 52

409. Keres–Spassky, Göteborg, 1955.
    1 Q×g7+!! K×g7 2 N×d7+ Kg8 3 Nf6+ Kf7 4 Nd5+ Kf8 5 N×c7 Resigns.
410. Nezhmetdinov–Estrin, Baku, 1951.
    1 N×g7!! K×g7 2 Nd4 Qc8 3 Nf5+ Kg8 4 Qg3+ Ng4 5 Q×g4+ Resigns.
411. Keres–Unzicker, Hamburg, 1956.
    1 N×g7!! R×g7 (if *1 ... Raf8 2 Ne6! R×f5 3 Qg4+ Kh8 4 N×f8*, or *1 ... K×g7 2 Bh6+! Kg8 3 Qg4+ Kh8 4 Qd4+*) 2 Bh6 Qe7 3 B×g7 Q×g7 (*3 ... K×g7 4 Qc3+ Kg8 5 Rf3*) 4 h4 h6 5 Rc4 Resigns.
412. Keller–Pomar, Lugano, 1968.
    1 B×g7! Re8+ 2 Kf1 B×g7 3 Q×f7+ Kh8 4 Qh5+ Kg8 5 Qh7+ Kf8 6 Ne6+!! Resigns (*6 ... R×e6 7 R×g7*).
413. Popova–Kasinova, Moscow, 1974.
    1 h×g6 f×g6 2 Q×h7+! K×h7 3 Rh1+ Resigns (on *3 ... Kg8* there comes *4 Rh8+ Kf7 5 Ng5* mate).
414. Flohr–Rovner, Tartu, 1950.
    1 R×h7+! N×h7 2 Rh1 Kg8 3 Q×h7+ Kf8 4 Ng6+ Resigns.
415. Totschalk–Alef, Corr., 1966.
    1 B×h7+!! K×h7 2 Qh5+ Kg8 3 Nc6!! g6 4 Qh6! Resigns.
416. Barda–Foltys, Marianske-Lazne, 1951.
    1 R×h7+!! R×h7 2 Qc8+ Kg7 3 Qg8+ Resigns (*3 ... Kh6 4 g5+*).

Test 53   Positions 417–424

A continuation of the preceding theme, but a rather more difficult test. Therefore the time allowed is 65 minutes.

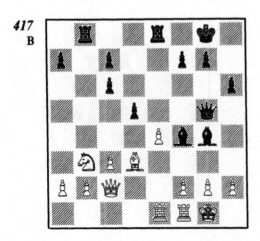

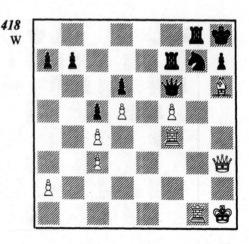

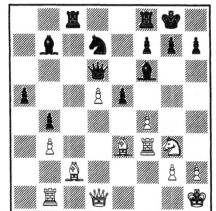

419
W

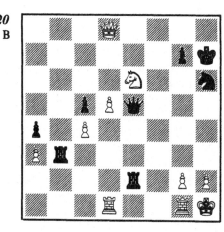

420
B

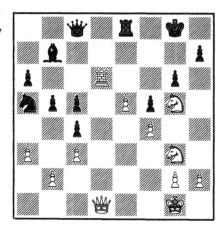

421
W

422
B

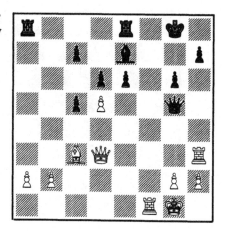

423
W

424
W

Solutions to Test 53

417. Koshel–Sheyanov, Sochi, 1971.
     1 ... B×h2+!! 2 K×h2 Bf3! 3 g×f3 Qh5+ 4 Kg2 Qg6+! White resigns. Against 5 ...
     Re5 and 6 ... Rh5 mate there is no defence.
418. Besser–Haakert, West Germany, 1969.
     1 Bg5! Qe5 2 Q×h7+!! K×h7 3 Rh4+ Nh5 4 R×h5+ Kg7 5 Be7 mate.
419. Belkadi–Littleton, Lugano, 1968.
     1 B×h7+! K×h7 2 Ne4 Q×d5 3 Rh3+ Kg8 4 Qh5 Resigns.
420. Polvin–Kreichik, Vienna, 1954.
     1 ... Q×h2+!! 2 K×h2 Ng4+ 3 Kh1 Rh3+! 4 g×h3 Rh2 mate.
421. Koszoru–Takacs, Hungary, 1952.
     1 N×h7! K×h7 2 R×g6! K×g6 3 Qh5+ Kg7 4 N×f5+ Resigns. If 4 ... Q×f5, then
     5 Q×f5 Bc6 6 Qf6+ Kg8 7 f5 Rf8 8 Qg6+ Kh8 9 f6 Rf8 10 Qh6 mate.
422. Sax–Farago, Budapest, 1974.
     1 ... R×h2+!! 2 K×h2 Rh8+ 3 Bh3 R×h3+!! 4 K×h3 Bd7+ White resigns.
423. Kuznetsov–Bichurin, Sverdlovsk, 1962.
     1 R×h7! K×h7 (or *1 ... e5 2 Rff7!*) 2 Rf7+ Kh6 3 Qh3+ Qh4 4 Bd2+ Bg5 5 Q×h4
     mate.
424. Matanovic–Nedeljkovic, Belgrade, 1950.
     1 B×h7+!! K×h7 2 Qh5+ Kg8 3 R×g7+! K×g7 4 Rg1+ Kf6 5 f5! Resigns.

Test 54   Positions 425–432

Another test on the same theme. Solving time—80 minutes.

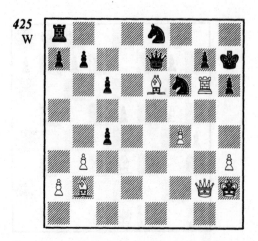

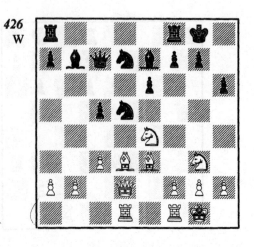

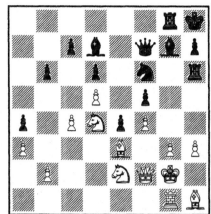

427
B

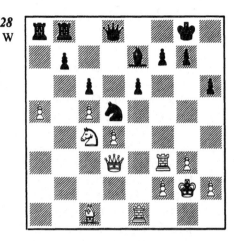

428
W

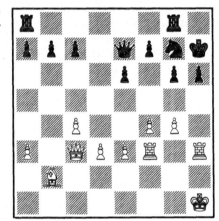

429
W

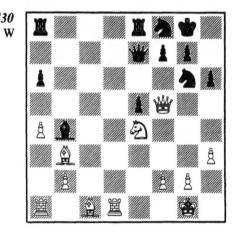

430
W

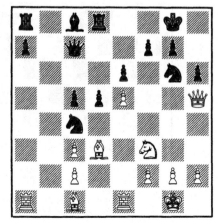

431
W

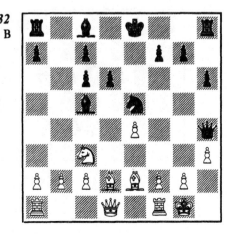

432
B

Solutions to Test 54

425. Bauer–Gelner, Berlin, 1956.
     1 R×h6+!! g×h6 (*1 ... K×h6 is no better: 2 Qg5+ Kh7 3 Qh4+ Kg6 4 f5 mate*) 2 Qg8+!! N×g8 3 Bf5 mate.

426. Zinn–Pietzsch, East Germany, 1961.
     1 B×h6! g×h6 2 Q×h6 Rfb8 (*2 ... Nf6 3 Ng5!*) 3 Nd6! Resigns (if *3 ... Nf6 4 Nh5!*).

427. Koleda–Dauga, Balvy, 1974.
     1 ... R×h3!! 2 K×h3 Qh5+ 3 Kg2 Ng4! White resigns.

428. Barcza–Zimmermann, Venice, 1949.
     1 B×h6!! g×h6 2 R×f7! K×f7 3 Ne5+ Kf8 4 Qh7, and White wins.

429. Heider–Kaller, Vienna, 1959.
     1 R×h6+!! K×h6 2 Q×g7++!! R×g7 3 Rh3+ Qh4 4 R×h4 mate.

430. Suetin–Nielsen, Copenhagen, 1965.
     1 B×h6!! g×h6 2 Rd7! N×d7 (or *2 ... Q×d7 3 Nf6+*) 3 Q×g6+ Kf8 (or *3 ... Kh8 4 B×f7!*) 4 Qh7! Resigns. On the only move 4 ... Nf6 there follows 5 Q×h6+ Kg8 6 N×f6+.

431. Hartston–Portisch, Nice, 1974.
     1 B×h6!! g×h6 2 Q×h6 Nb2 3 Ng5 N×d3 (if *3 ... Nf8, then 4 Bh7+ N×h7 5 N×h7 f5 6 Nf6+ Kf7 7 Qh7+ Kf8 8 Qg8+ Ke7 9 Qg7 mate*) 4 Nh7! Resigns.

432. Den–Mahle, Dortmund, 1964.
     1 ... B×h3!! 2 g×h3 (no better is *2 Bf1 Bg4!*) 2 ... Qg3+ 3 Kh1 Q×h3+ 4 Kg1 g5! (this is stronger than *4 ... Qg3+ 5 Kh1 B×f2*) 5 Be3 g4 White resigns.

Test 55   Positions 433–440

Another test on the theme of 'Destructive combinations'. The time allowed is 70 minutes.

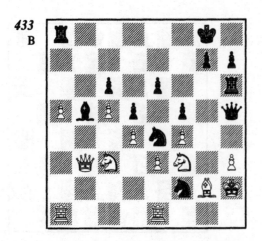

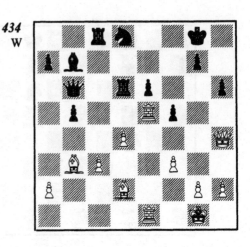

435
W

436
W

437
W

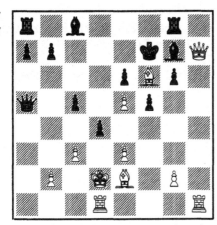

438
W

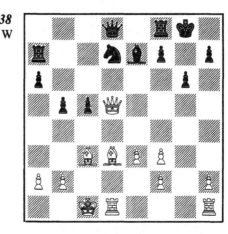

439
W

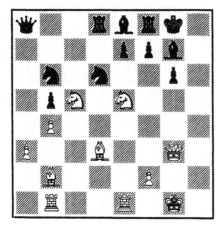

440
W

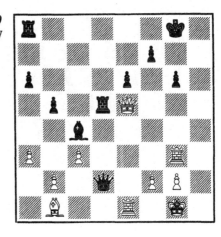

Solutions to Test 55

433. Ivanov–Karastoichev, Plovdiv, 1952.

1 ... Q×h3+!! 2 B×h3 R×h3+ 4 Kg2 Rg3+ 4 Kh2 Ng4+ 5 Kh1 Nef2 mate.

434. Szabo–Portisch, Budapest, 1959.

1 B×h6! g×h6 2 Q×h6 R×c3 3 Qg6+ Kh8 (or *3 Kf8 4 R×f5+!*) 4 R×f5! Q×d4+ 5 Kh1 Resigns.

435. Pomar–Robatsch, Palma de Mallorca, 1966.

1 N×h6+! g×h6 2 Qf6 Ng6 3 Q×d6 Nh4 4 Rd2 Qe3+ 5 Rdf2 Resigns.

436. Deimer–Illini, Corr., 1954/55.

1 B×g6!! (the immediate *1 Bg7* does not work on account of *1 ... Q×d4+ 2 Kh1 N×d3*) 1 ... f×g6 2 Bg7!! Nc6 (*2 ... K×g7 loses to 3 Qh6+ Kg8 4 R×f6!*) 3 N×c6 b×c6 4 Qh6 Nh5 5 R×h5! Resigns.

437. Maryasin–Kapengut, Minsk, 1969.

1 Q×g6+!! K×g6 2 Bh5+ Kh7 3 Bf7+ Bh6 4 R×h6+! Resigns.

438. Meyer–Unger, Corr., 1957.

1 Rhg1 Nf6 2 B×g6! h×g6 (*2 ... N×d5 3 Be4+ Bg5 4 R×d5!*, or *2 ... Q×d5 3 Be4+ Kh8 4 R×d5*) 3 R×g6+ Kh7 4 Rg7+! Resigns.

439. Vasyukov–Zhelyandinov, Kharkov, 1967.

1 N×g6!! f×g6 2 B×g7 K×g7 3 R×e7+ Rf7 4 Ne6+ Kh8 5 R×f7 Resigns. On 5 ... N×f7 there follows 6 Q×g6, while if 5 ... B×f7, then 6 Qe5+ Kh7 7 Qg7 mate.

440. Timoshchenko–Mikhalchishin, Tbilisi, 1973.

1 R×g6+!! f×g6 2 Q×e6+ Kg7 3 Q×g6+ Kf8 4 Qf6+ Kg8 5 Bh7+! Resigns.

Test 56   Positions 441–448

The final test on this theme, for which 70 minutes are allowed.

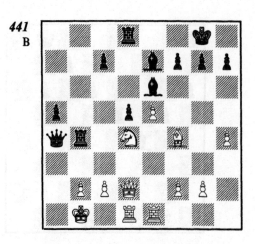

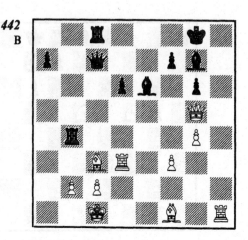

443
B

444
B

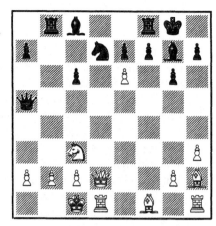

445
B

446
B

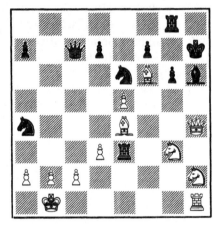

447
W

448
W

Solutions to Test 56

441. Tolush–Vasiliev, Leningrad, 1945.

1 ... R×b2+! 2 K×b2 Qa3+ 3 Kb1 Rb8+ 4 Nb3 R×b3+! White resigns (on *5 c×b3* there follows *5 ... Bf5+ 6 Qd3 Q×b3+ 7 Ka1 B×d3*).

442. Shevelev–Venediktov, Sverdlovsk, 1957.

1 ... R×b2!! 2 K×b2 B×c3+ 3 Kc1 Bf6 4 Qd2 Bg5!! White resigns.

443. Podolny–Sopkov, Yaroslavl, 1948.

1 ... R×b2!! 2 B×f5 (*2 K×b2* loses to *2 ... Q×c3+ 3 Kc1 Rb8!*, when there is no defence against *4 ... Rb1+ 5 K×b1 Qb2* mate) 2 ... Rfb8 3 Bg4 Q×c3 4 R×c3 B×c3 White resigns.

444. Wilkung–Inbrand, Göteborg, 1973.

1 ... R×b2!! 2 e×d7 (or *2 K×b2 Qb4+ 3 Kc1 B×c3*) 2 ... B×c3 3 d8=Q Rb1+! 4 K×b1 Qb4+ 5 Kc1 Qb2 mate.

445. Sajtar–Szabo, Bucharest, 1953.

1 ... N×f3!! 2 R×f3 Qe4 3 Qd1 h5! (if *3 ... R×f3*, then *4 Q×f3 Q×b1 5 Q×d5+*) 4 g×h5 Rf5! White resigns.

446. Teschner–Darga, Alkmar, 1953.

1 ... Re1+!! 2 R×e1 Q×c2+!! 3 K×c2 Nd4+ 4 Kb1 Nc3+ 5 b×c3 (or *5 Ka1 Nc2* mate) 5 ... Rb8+ 6 Ka1 Nc2 mate.

447. Khailibeili–Solntsev, Moscow, 1964.

1 R×c6!! R×c7 (or *1 ... N×c6 2 R×a6+ b×a6 3 B×c6* mate) 2 Rc×a6+ Kb8 3 Ra8 mate.

448. Muslimova–Voskresenskaya, Tashkent, 1960.

1 R×a6!! b×a6 2 Nf6!! Kb8 3 N×d7+ Resigns.

Progress Chart

Test No.	Basic Score (max 40)	Time Taken (mins.)	Net Score	Comments
1		(75)		
2		(70)		
3		(75)		
4		(80)		
5		(60)		
6		(60)		
7		(60)		
8		(60)		
9		(60)		
10		(60)		
11		(60)		
12		(60)		
13		(60)		
14		(70)		
15		(60)		
16		(50)		
17		(70)		
18		(75)		
19		(65)		
20		(70)		
21		(75)		
22		(60)		
23		(60)		
24		(55)		
25		(65)		
26		(75)		
27		(50)		
28		(70)		
29		(60)		
30		(75)		
31		(60)		
32		(60)		
33		(65)		
34		(80)		

35		(90)	
36		(55)	
37		(50)	
38		(50)	
39		(55)	
40		(60)	
41		(60)	
42		(55)	
43		(70)	
44		(45)	
45		(45)	
46		(75)	
47		(70)	
48		(70)	
49		(70)	
50		(70)	
51		(60)	
52		(60)	
53		(65)	
54		(80)	
55		(70)	
56		(70)	

Index of Players